Authentic Recipes from
THAILAND

recipes by Sven Krauss, Laurent Ganguillet and Vira Sanguanwong
photographs by Luca Invernizzi Tettoni

PERIPLUS

Published by Periplus Editions with editorial offices at
130 Joo Seng Road #06-01
Singapore 368357
Tel (65) 6280-1330; fax (65) 6280-6290
Email: inquiries@periplus.com.sg
Website: www.periplus.com

Hardcover ISBN: 0-7946-0210-X
Paperback ISBN: 0-7946-0207-X
Printed in Singapore

Distributed by

North America, Latin America and Europe
Tuttle Publishing, 364 Innovation Drive,
North Clarendon, VT 05759-9436
Tel: (802) 773-8930; fax: (802) 773-6993
Email: info@tuttlepublishing.com

Japan and Korea
Tuttle Publishing, Yaekari Building, 3F
5-4-12 Osaki, Shinagawa-ku, Tokyo 141-0032
Tel: (03) 5437-0171; fax: (03) 5437-0755
Email: tuttle-sales@gol.com

Asia Pacific
Berkeley Books Pte Ltd
130 Joo Seng Road #06-01/03
Singapore 368357
Tel (65) 6280-1330; fax (65) 6280-6290
Email: inquiries@periplus.com.sg

Photographer: Luca Invernizzi Tettoni
Food stylists and recipe testers: Sven Krauss,
Laurent Ganguillet and Vira Sanguanwong

Contents

The Food of Thailand
International acclaim for Asia's most popular cuisine

Images of Thailand among outsiders vary according to taste and temperament. To some, the country conjures up a *King and I* fantasy of gilded temples and palaces, to others a palm-fringed beach of snowy white sand, an exotic tribal village high in misty mountains or the brassy, big-city lure of Bangkok. All are valid enough as individual impressions, yet misleading in terms of the whole, for Thailand, like its food, is a complex mixture of flavors and the product of a unique history.

Covering some 198,500 square miles (514,100 square kilometers)—roughly the size of France—it encompasses a wide range of topography. Mountains in the far north, where Thailand's borders meet those of Burma and Laos, rise to more than 8,000 feet (2,500 meters), with verdant valleys and the remains of once-extensive teak forests.

The northeast consists of a rolling, semi-arid plateau stretching all the way to the Mekong River, while the flat central plains, watered by the Chao Phraya River, form one of the richest rice-growing regions on earth. The narrow southern isthmus, extending down to Malaysia, is bordered on one side by the Gulf of Thailand and on the other by the Indian Ocean, with a spine of rugged limestone mountains down the middle.

A largely benign climate allows year-round cultivation of crops, not only rice but also fruits and vegetables. Even today, despite the growth of urban areas, the great majority of the population can be found in rural villages of around 150 households (about 700 people) who derive their living from agriculture. Other natural resources include a variety of minerals, precious stones, such as rubies and sapphires, and an abundance of seafood along two long coastlines bordering the Indian Ocean to the west and the South China Sea to the east.

A Land of Plenty

The Thais were not the first people drawn to this land of plenty. Evidence of settlers dating back to the Paleolithic Age, some 500,000 years ago, has been found in several parts of the country, and archaeologists exploring a cave near the Burmese border discovered the carbonized remains of such plants as Chinese water chestnut, bottle gourd and cucumber that were dated from 9,700 to 6,000 B.C. The most dramatic and extensive prehistoric remains have emerged in the northeast, where a remarkable culture flourished from around 4,000 B.C. to just after the start of the Common Era, numbering among its achievements rice cultivation and sophisticated bronze metallurgy.

Indian traders later established ports along the southern peninsula, bringing not only Buddhism but numerous other cultural and culinary influences. Mon settlers arrived around the same time in the Chao Phraya valley and founded the Dvaravati kingdom, a major producer of rice as well as an important religious center. Their power was eventually replaced by that of the Khmers, whose empire once extended over the northeast and central regions.

Rice culture came with the earliest settlers, long before the Thais themselves arrived on the scene, and led to a vast complex of paddy fields watered by an intricate system of canals, rivers and reservoirs.

The ethnic Thais, originating as a minority group in what is now southern China, gradually migrated southward in search of greater independence and better land for agriculture. The earliest groups settled in the far north, forming a loose federation of city states centered around Chiang Mai. Others ventured farther south, to the northern extremities of the central plains. By the 13th century, the Thais had established themselves in such numbers that they were eventually able to overthrow their Khmer overlords and establish a kingdom of their own.

This kingdom was called Sukhothai, which in Sanskrit means "Dawn of Happiness," and though its power lasted less than two centuries, its influence proved far more enduring. Under King Ramkhamhaeng, the greatest Sukhothai ruler, the Thai alphabet was devised, splendid works of Buddhist art were created and a truly indigenous Thai culture emerged.

"In the water there are fish, in the fields there is rice." This celebrated stone inscription is credited to King Ramkhamhaeng of Sukhothai, the first independent Thai kingdom founded in the early 13th century. The inscription testifies to a natural abundance that was to sustain a series of capitals down the length of Thailand's fertile Chao Phraya River valley and more specifically, to the two staples of the Thai diet since then—rice and fish.

To these basic ingredients, readily available to all, were gradually added others, drawn over the centuries from a wide variety of cultures: some nearby, like China and India, some remote like Persia and Portugal. Even such seemingly essential elements as the pungent chili pepper were, in fact, introductions from distant South America. However they came, though, they were subtly modified and refined into a cuisine distinctively Thai, not quite like any other in the world.

The diverse glories of classic Thai cooking long remained unappreciated by the outside world. Alone among the countries of Southeast Asia, Thailand remained

LEFT: A table for two is more likely to be found in a restaurant than in a family home, where dining is a sociable experience shared by many.

The Food of Thailand 5

independent during the era of colonization; thus, relatively few Westerners sampled its unique blends of hot and sweet, sour and salty—so different from the dishes of India, Malaya and Indonesia, despite superficial similarities.

Even those who came for lengthy stays were rarely treated to the genuine fare. Restaurants catering to foreigners in larger cities like Bangkok tended until quite recently to be Chinese or European. For the most part, only in private homes could one sample delicate, traditional dishes that resulted from hours of preparation by skilled hands, using methods that had been handed down for generations.

All that, of course, has now changed dramatically. In the past two decades, Thai food has become an international phenomenon, with countless restaurants now offering it, from Sydney to Stockholm.

Serious Western chefs find fresh inspiration in its flavors and techniques, and ordinary diners are discovering its remarkable diversity. In Thailand itself, regional variations are far more available than before, and there are now elegantly decorated establishments specializing in the refined art of "palace cooking."

Thai food, then, might be said to have entered a new era, one that will certainly bring an even wider appreciation of its many delights.

Despite the popularity of Thai cuisine, many people do not appreciate the true extent of its diversity. Perhaps the majority of foreign lovers of Thai food have acquired their taste for it in restaurants abroad, or during a visit limited largely to Bangkok. What many may fail to realize is that the country's cooking varies from region to region, sometimes in small ways that only a true expert could fully appreciate, sometimes in dramatic ways. A provincial journey can thus be a rewarding culinary experience as well as an opportunity to enjoy a variety of scenic attractions.

In the mountainous north, for instance, where borders are shared with Burma and Laos, the cuisine is as distinctive as the handicrafts for which the region is noted. Here, the earliest Thais settled on their migration southward from China, forming first a group of small city states and then a loose federation known as Lanna, with Chiang Mai as the principal city. Over the years there were conflicts with both Burma and the rising Thai state of Ayutthaya in the Central Plains. Even after the Lanna kingdom came under the administrative control of Bangkok, it remained remote from the rest of the country until a railway was cut in 1921.

As a result of this long isolation, the north was able to retain much of its native culture: its language (as different from central Thai as Spanish is from Portuguese), its crafts

Kantoke, a meal taken while seated on the floor of the house around a low round table, is a traditional way of dining in the north of Thailand.

Feasting in the Streets

First come the pile drivers to lay the foundations for one of the huge new buildings that seem to be rising on almost every street corner in Bangkok and other major cities. The workers follow, setting up a collection of temporary shacks on or near the site. And then, often simultaneously, the food vendors appear, ready to supply a quick, inexpensive and above all convenient meal to anyone who happens to crave one.

Amidst the aroma of charcoal fires and cooked foods, Thailand's street vendors sell an impressive variety of food. Customers can sit down to enjoy their meal and watch the unfolding street scene whilst adding to the colorful mosaic themselves. A Thai city street without food vendors is as hard to imagine as one devoid of traffic.

As a result of this widespread interest, Thai street food has evolved into a distinctive culinary category all its own, generally characterized by speed of preparation (if any is done on the spot) and easy portability of equipment. It can be divided into two categories: snacks and more substantial fare, meaning that one can buy what amounts to a multi-course meal without setting foot in a restaurant.

Snacks come in various shapes and sizes. Some may consist of nothing more than freshly sliced fruit sprinkled with salt, sugar, dried chilies or a combination of these seasonings. Others may be a selection of traditional sweets, prepared by the vendor at home and temptingly arranged in a display case.

Other vendors offer noodle creations adequate for a fast, nourishing lunch. To produce the universally popular kwaytiaow soup, a bowl of freshly cooked rice noodles is given a few ladles of meat stock, then topped with precooked pork or chicken, and sprinkled with sugar, crushed peanuts and dried chili flakes, while for Pad Thai the noodles are quickly stir-fried with garlic, spring onions, dried shrimp, tamarind and a variety of spices. Gai Yang, northeastern-style barbecued chicken, is grilled over a charcoal brazier and served with side orders of glutinous rice and green papaya salad.

Just about every governor of Bangkok has tried, at some point in their tenure, to outlaw the city's food vendors. General untidiness, civic hygiene and even sidewalk obstruction are among the reasons cited for banishing Bangkok's colorful street vendors.

However, all have failed for the simple reason that the vendors fill a clearly perceived need for a substantial number of Bangkok's residents. Take away the opportunity for Thais to enjoy a quick, delicious meal and, as one irate fan wrote indignantly to a local newspaper, "it would be the end of civilization as we know it."

ABOVE: Duck Noodle Soup, a popular streetside favorite.
BELOW: An artist's impression of "food to go" in Thailand, where pushcarts and street stalls are an essential part of everyday life.

Culinary Arts of the Thai Palace

The innermost part of Bangkok's Grand Palace, where the women of the court lived, was known as the "Inside." At its peak, during the reign of King Rama V, the "Inside" had a population of nearly 3,000—a select few of them bearing the exalted rank of Queen but the great majority being ladies-in-waiting and lower attendants. Many foreigners viewed the "Inside" as the most obvious manifestation of polygamy, an institution they disapproved of. The inner palace can perhaps be more accurately viewed as an ultra-exclusive finishing school, where the most refined aristocratic skills were perfected and passed on. The daughter of a nobleman who had spent all or part of her youth in this rarefied atmosphere was regarded as highly desirable by any future husband, for she would be adept at supervising an elegant household of her own in the outside world.

During their ample leisure time, the royal women learned such delicate arts as traditional Thai floral decoration, threading fragrant blossoms into intricate wreaths and molding clay into miniature dolls of marvellous detail. Above all, they learned how to prepare various foods that were not merely more subtle in flavor than their outside versions but highly memorable in visual appeal.

The hallmarks of the so-called "palace food" were painstaking hours of preparation and an artistic sense of presentation. Foi Thong, for instance, is a blend of egg yolks and sugar transformed into a nest of silky golden threads, while Look Choop are tiny imitation fruits shaped by hand from a mixture of bean paste and coconut milk and colored to match their real-life models. Mee Grob, which one writer has called "the epitome of palace cuisine," involves crisp rice noodles and shrimp in a sweet-sour sauce, so time-consuming to make properly that it was once seldom found in restaurants.

Fruit and vegetable carving was the most visible of these palace skills. Watermelons, spring onions, mangoes, ginger root and other garnishes and delicacies became intricately carved flowers, leaves, and abstract designs through the deft use of a knife, sometimes taking longer to prepare than the dishes they adorned.

Royal polygamy ended under King Rama VI and the royal women and their attendants gradually left their protected existence and made new lives for themselves outside the palace walls.

Fortunately, Thailand's palace cooking did not vanish along with the hidden world where it originated. It survived through the descendants of the royal women and, especially in recent years, has been discovered by a wider public through several restaurants that take great pride in their re-creations of this uniquely fascinating cuisine.

ABOVE: Five-colored porcelain or *Bencharong* wares seen in the foreground of a corner of Vimarn Mek Palace were originally created in China to meet Thai tastes, but are now produced in Thailand.
LEFT: Hours of painstaking effort and great skill are needed to produce the exquisite fruit and vegetable carvings which are a hallmark of palace cuisine.

Nam Prik Ong, a spicy pork and tomato dip, surrounded by raw vegetables, salted duck egg and crispy pork skin.

(among them lacquer, silverware and fine woodcarving), its customs (such as placing a jar of cool water outside houses for thirsty passersby) and its food.

Instead of the soft, boiled rice of the central region, northerners prefer a steamed glutinous variety, rolled into small balls and dipped into liquid dishes. Curries of the region tend to be thinner, without the coconut milk so widely used in central and southern cooking. There is also a distinctive local version of Nam Prik Ong, a basic dipping sauce served with raw vegetables and crispy pork skin, as well as a pork sausage called Naem, eaten plain with rice or mixed into various dishes. When it is in season, the favorite local fruit is the succulent *longan*, which grows in almost every compound.

Regional Styles and Foreign Influences

The influence of neighboring Burma and Laos is apparent in many northern dishes. The former, for example, was responsible for the popular Khao Soi, a curry broth with egg noodles and chicken, pork or beef, as well as Gaeng Hang Lay, a pork curry seasoned with ginger, tamarind and turmeric. Of Laotian origin are Nam Prik Noom, a sauce with a strong chili-lime flavor and Ook Gai, a red chicken curry with lemongrass.

The traditional form of entertainment in the north is the *kantoke* dinner, the name derived from *kan*, or "bowl," and *toke*, a low round table made of woven bamboo, plain or lacquered. Sitting on the floor around the table, guests help themselves to the assorted dishes placed on it and regularly replenished by the attentive hostess.

Like the north, northeastern Thailand was also long regarded as remote from the cosmopolitan world of Bangkok. In this case, however, the reason was not so much geography as a perceptible social prejudice on the part of city dwellers. Isan, as Thais call the northeast, was the poorest of the country's four main regions, with infertile soil and devastating droughts that frequently drove farmers to the capital in search of work as laborers, taxi drivers and domestic servants.

Finicky outsiders tended to look on Isan food as "strange," and some of the region's delicacies are certainly unusual when compared with the abundance of other areas: grubworms and grasshoppers, for instance, ant eggs, snail curry and fermented fish of exceptional pungency. But increasingly, other less exotic dishes typical of the region have won widespread admiration, to the point where they now appear on the menus of smart Bangkok restaurants and are savored by the most discriminating Thai food connoisseurs. Some diners, indeed, look upon a properly prepared Som Tam (spicy green papaya salad) or Laab (even spicier minced pork or chicken) as being the true marks of a superior Thai cook, wherever he may be plying his trade.

If the people of Isan "eat anything," as residents of other regions often remark, they have a definite skill for transforming it in ways that show both imagination and ingenuity.

Barbecued chicken or Gai Yang, is grilled with a healthy lashing of peppery sauce and garlic, while catfish is the base of a delectable curry, and Laab Dip is made with raw meat and roasted rice powder.

For Haw Mok, fish is ground with curry paste and then steamed in banana leaf to make a many-flavored custard. Beef—a relatively rare commodity—is marinated and grilled, and any leftovers are combined with fresh mint, green onions and chilies for a fiery salad. Perhaps because chilies add such a zip to the most mundane dish, northeasterners tend to use them with a greater abandon than Thais of other areas.

Much northeastern cooking reflects the influence of Laos just across the Mekong River—not surprisingly since many residents are ethnically Lao. Dill (called *pak chee Lao* or "Laotian coriander" by Thais) is widely used as a garnish, and glutinous rice is preferred to the normal variety. Also of Lao origin and popular on festive occasions is Khanom Buang, a crispy crepe stuffed with dried shrimp, bean sprouts, and other ingredients.

Southern Thailand consists of a slender peninsula stretching down to Malaysia, dramatically different from the rest of the country in both scenery and culture. Lush jungle clambers up craggy limestone mountains, nurtured by rain that falls for eight months of the year, and cultivated areas tend to be vast rubber and coconut plantations rather than the familiar rice fields and fruit orchards of the central plains. From villages along two long coastlines—one on the Gulf of Thailand, the other on the Indian Ocean—thousands of boats sail out to fish the surrounding waters, bringing back seafood for local consumption and profitable export.

Highly distinctive visually is the domed mosque, for the south is home to most of Thailand's two million Muslims, its largest religious minority. These are concentrated in the provinces adjacent to Malaysia, where Malay is spoken as commonly as Thai. In other southern places like Songkhla and the island of Phuket, Chinese predominate and lend their own particular color to the local scene.

Southern food reflects most of these features, cultural and otherwise, as well as others from its more distant past when traders from India and Sumatra sailed to its numerous ports. The graceful coconuts to be seen growing so plentifully everywhere provide milk for thickening soups and curries, oil for frying, and grated flesh as a condiment for many dishes.

From the seas come huge marine fish, rock lobsters, crabs, mussels, squid, prawns and scallops, while local plantations yield cashew nuts, which turn up regularly as an appetizer or garnish, and small but juicy pineapples, which provide a popular sweet at the end of a meal.

Seafood may be prepared simply, grilled or steamed; or more elaborately, baked in a claypot with thin noodles and garlic; or as the main component of Tom Yam, that ubiquitous Thai soup laced with lemongrass and chilies. In general, southerners like their food chili-hot, and are fond of a bitter taste imparted by a flat, native bean called *sa-taw*, which other Thais tend to find less appealing.

Contributions from other cultures include Gaeng Mussaman, an Indian-style curry with cardamom, cloves, cinnamon and either chicken or beef; Malay fish curries, often with a garnish of tamarind and fresh fruit; and Indonesian satay, marinated bits of meat on bamboo skewers with a spicy peanut sauce.

The fourth of the country's regions, the Central Plains, is the Thai heartland: a vast checkerboard of paddy fields, orchards and vegetable gardens, with Bangkok as the principal market and cultural magnet. The best rice comes from here, pearly white and fragrant, and so do the best fruits—mangoes and durians, ruby-red mangosteens and hairy rambutans, crisp guavas, papayas and pomelos, even grapes in a special tropical hybrid. Vegetables, eaten in large quantities, include cabbage, mushrooms, morning glory (water spinach), cucumber, tomatoes and pumpkins, as well as more recent introductions like asparagus and baby corn.

Food in the villages that stand like islands amid the fields tends to be plain: rice with stir-fried vegetables, fish from a nearby canal or river, perhaps some minced chicken with garlic, chilies and basil and a salad of salted eggs, chilies and spring onion with a squeeze of lime.

The Evolution of Thai Cuisine
The development of a unique and skillfully composed mosaic

One of the most notable characteristics of Thai decorative art is its passion for intricate detail, particularly apparent in complex mosaics of colored glass and porcelain that adorn so many religious buildings. From afar, these suggest a solid, seamless pattern; only on closer inspection are the separate components revealed, and the skillful way they have been put together.

It is easy to see an analogy between such mosaics and many aspects of Thai culture, including its cuisine. Here, too, a wide variety of elements has been brought together and artfully composed into something quite unique, often surprising in the effect that it creates.

Little is known about the cooking of Sukhothai, where so much of what we regard as distinctively Thai first emerged. From the information in King Ramkhamhaeng's famous inscription, however, it is clear that rice and fish were the major ingredients. Fruits were undoubtedly plentiful as well, along with mushrooms that grew wild in the forests and a variety of vegetables. One item not present, however, was the now ubiquitous chili, which originated in Central and South America and did not appear in Asian cuisines until the arrival of the first Europeans, several centuries later.

A clearer picture is available of Ayutthaya, thanks largely to 17th-century French visitors who characteristically devoted a considerable amount of space to the subject of food in their accounts of the kingdom. Simon de la Loubere, for instance, who came with a diplomatic mission in 1687, was struck by the fact that the people ate sparingly. Good salt, he found, was a rare commodity, and fresh fish was seldom eaten, despite its abundance.

"A Siamese," he wrote, "makes a very good meal with a pound of rice a day, which amounts to not more than a farthing, and with a little dry or salt fish, which costs not much more...Their sauces are plain, a little water with some spices, garlic, or some sweet herb. They do very much esteem a liquid sauce, like mustard, which is only crayfish corrupted because they are ill-salted; they call it *kapi*."

Nicolas Gervaise, a Jesuit missionary, noted that *kapi*, the popular fermented shrimp paste, "has such a pungent smell that it nauseates anyone not accustomed to it" and gives perhaps the first general recipe for a typical Thai condiment based on it: "salt, pepper, ginger, cinnamon, cloves, garlic, white onions, nutmeg and several strongly flavored herbs...mixed in considerable quantities with this shrimp paste."

From these accounts it is clear that for all its seeming simplicity, Thai cooking was already becoming more sophisticated. The presence of cloves and nutmeg is evidence of trade with the East Indies, and the fact that

numerous Chinese, Japanese, Malays and Indians lived in Ayutthaya suggests other likely influences. None of the French writers specifically mentions chilies, but they were probably already in use, either brought directly by the Portuguese, who opened relations in 1511, or having come via Malacca or India. The Portuguese were also responsible for a number of still popular Thai sweets based on sugar and egg yolks and possibly for introducing the tomato, which is of New World origin.

The complex seasonings we now regard as typical of Thai cuisine, including chilies, were certainly well established by the Rattanakosin, or Bangkok, period. This is made abundantly clear in an account by Sir John Bowring, who wrote in 1855: "The Siamese prepare considerable quantities of curry as their habitual food. These are generally so hot that they burn the mouth of a European."

Bowring obviously learned to appreciate some of the "ardent comestibles," among them the essential sauce called *nam prik*, which, he explained, "is prepared by bruising a small quantity of red pepper in a mortar, to which are added *kapi* (paste of shrimps or prawns), black pepper, garlic and onions. These being thoroughly mixed, a small quantity of brine and citron-juice is added. Ginger, tamarinds and gourd seeds are also employed. The *nam prik* is one of the most appetite-exciting condiments."

Rice noodles were probably common in Ayutthaya, part of China's considerable culinary legacy, but they became even more so in Bangkok, enhanced with Thai flavors and popular as a luncheon dish. Vendors offered a quick meal of *kwaytiaow* (stir-fried noodles with vegetables and meat or shrimp) from boats along the canals that threaded the capital and still do on almost every sidewalk in the city.

Thai food today may still be plain or fancy, a dish that can be prepared in a few minutes over a charcoal brazier or one requiring hours of chopping, grinding and carving; it may vary considerably from region to region. Always, though, it remains a singular creation, not quite like any of the influences that have shaped it over the centuries.

RIGHT: Herbal medicines are still prepared according to prescriptions preserved in ancient Thai manuscripts.

Eating and Cooking Thai
Preparing and enjoying an authentic Thai meal

Of the various basic implements used in the preparation of Thai food, a number have remained essentially unchanged over the years. Others have been replaced by more efficient modern devices and are now mainly to be seen in antique shops, objects admired for their beauty of form but not serving a practical purpose for the modern Thai cook.

In a traditional Thai home of the not-very-distant past, the kitchen was nearly always a separate structure from the main house, its central feature being an often smoky stove. Lacking gas or electricity, the fuel was usually charcoal, or wood where it was readily available, as in forested areas like the north. There are still many noted Thai cooks who insist that only charcoal can provide the desired quality of heat for certain dishes and who maintain a small brazier along with the gas and electric cookers that have become standard equipment, at least in city households.

The oldest kind of stove used in Thailand, now virtually extinct, was an ingenious device called a *cherng kran*, a rimmed earthenware tray with one side raised to hold the bottom of a cooking pot. The fuel was placed under the pot on the tray. This had the advantages of requiring little space and of being easily moved from place. The *cherng kran* later gave way to somewhat more substantial, but still portable, charcoal cookers and finally to built-in ranges that were made of tiled cement, perhaps reflecting the tendency of the Thais themselves to stay put as more permanent towns and cities developed.

A Few Necessary Implements

The actual cooking of most Thai dishes, past and present, is done with remarkable speed and employs only a small number of utensils, the most important of them being a **wok**, a **spatula** with a rounded edge to stir the food around, and assorted **pots** for boiling.

Far more time, however, must be spent on the preliminary preparation of various ingredients, which have to be peeled, chopped, grated, ground, blended and marinated, essential procedures that can take several hours for some creations and that led to the evolution of many special tools. One of the most decorative of these was the *kude maprow* or coconut grater needed to prepare fresh coconut cream or milk. This utensil probably began as a simple seat, at one end of

which was a sharp iron grater and below this, a tray to receive the shredded coconut meat, all often carved from a single piece of wood. The user straddled the seat and, leaning forward, rotated half a coconut around the teeth of the grater in a process that looked easier than it actually was—the tiniest of slips could result in a painful cut. The *kude maprow* eventually became more elaborate, with the seat carved in various shapes, usually that of a rabbit (perhaps because of the protruding teeth) but also other animals or humans, and displaying considerable artistry. Today these utensils are comparatively rare and much sought after by collectors. However, coconut is today grated by machine in the market or with the use of a food processor at home. To save time, many cooks now rely on packaged or canned coconut cream.

Other classic implements have proved more durable than the coconut grater. The *krok* and *saak*, or mortar and pestle, traditionally made of stone or wood but also available in baked clay or metal, is still used to pound and grind spices that produce the distinctive flavors of Thai food. Usually there are two of these, a deep one for up and down pounding and a flat one for grinding.

TOP: High-tech alloys now replace cast iron as the favorite material for the wok.
BOTTOM LEFT: Different types of spatula for stirring can be used with a wok.
BOTTOM RIGHT: Traditional coconut scrapers are increasingly rare.
OPPOSITE: Northeastern or Isan food, once looked on with suspicion by other Thais, has now gained wide acceptance.

Although many traditionally-minded cooks swear that modern blenders and food processors cannot provide the same taste as a mortar and pestle, most cooks even in Thailand today are prepared to trade speed and ease of preparation for the laborious old method. When using a blender to grind items such as shallots, garlic and chilies, be sure to chop or slice all items first, and to blend the tougher ingredients before adding the softer ones. Add a little of the cooking medium (oil, coconut milk or water) specified in the recipe, to help keep the blades turning if necessary.

There are, however, no satisfactory substitutes for the thick wooden **chopping block** and sharp **cleaver** used in heavy-duty and delicate cutting. These are available in most Asian specialty stores.

Another important adjunct to the Thai kitchen is a **wire-mesh basket** with a long handle of wood or bamboo, used to lower foods into oil for deep-frying, to plunge noodles into boiling water and to blanch vegetables. These come in a number of forms, depending on the use—shallow for frying, deeper for holding noodles and vegetables, and are available at every market. (Similar items can be found in Western stores.)

Equally essential for preparing many basic dishes is some sort of **steamer**. Often today this is made of metal and may even be electric, though in provincial areas it is still more likely to be traditional—a set of bamboo trays, for instance, which are stacked over boiling water with a cover on the top one; or, in the north and northeast, an elegant footed utensil known as a *kong khao*, which can be used for steaming glutinous rice and also for carrying it while traveling or working in the fields.

In addition to these, there are more exotic devices difficult to find outside Thailand, each used for a very specific purpose. One, the *ka po*, consists of three-quarters of a coconut shell, in the bottom of which are drilled small holes; two parallel rods are attached with rattan to either side of the top so that the shell can be placed on a pot of boiling water. Rice-flour, tapioca, or mung bean paste is poured into the bowl and pressed to produce a noodle-like sweet, which is then sieved and served cold. A simpler variation is the *lachong*, a perforated metal plate that looks like a cheese grater, through which the paste is pressed.

Several brass or bronze implements are also used to make some of the more complex sweets. A cone with two small openings facilitates the production of Foi Thong, or "golden threads," a delicate egg-yolk creation thought to have been introduced by the Portuguese during the Ayutthaya period. A sauce dispenser with a small hole (such as the Kikkoman soy sauce bottle) makes an acceptable substitute, although it takes a fair amount of practice to create these "golden threads."

Another unusual utensil is a shell-shaped mold, usually made of brass, with a long wooden handle. The mold is dipped first into hot oil and then into batter; it is plunged back into the oil and the batter cooks to form delicate crisp little cups. These cups or *krathong* are filled to make delightful savory snacks. (Similar snacks known as *kuih pi tee* are found in neighboring Malaysia and Singapore.)

Some of these implements have now made their way into Western cookery shops specializing in Asian cuisine. While reasonable substitutes can be found for most of the others, the pleasure of a visit to Thailand can be enhanced by plunging into a colorful market and finding the genuine article, which can later be put to practical use.

The Thai Dining Experience

Wherever it is eaten—in a restaurant, on a city sidewalk, on the open verandah of a farm house, even in the middle of a rice field at harvest time—a Thai meal is nearly always a social affair. In most urban areas, a table and chairs are likely to be used for dining, though the floor, covered with soft reed mats, suffices in many rural homes. Moreover, Western cutlery has now come into general use: not knives, for in a properly prepared Thai meal nothing is large enough to need cutting, but a large spoon to scoop up individual portions of rice and a fork to help move the food on one's plate.

In the north and northeast, where steamed glutinous rice is preferred, the fingers are used to form small rice balls and dip them into more liquid dishes. Chopsticks may be provided for Chinese-style noodle dishes, and a ceramic Chinese spoon for soups and certain desserts.

A large container of rice is usually the centerpiece, either a wicker basket or an elaborately decorated covered bowl made of silver or pressed aluminium. Around this are placed the other dishes and condiments, and dessert, if one is served. Guests are free to help themselves, mixing dishes at will and seasoning them with a wide variety of condiments to achieve the desired taste. The soup may be eaten at either the beginning or the end of a meal, and the salad likewise. The only constants are the rice, which accompanies almost everything, and dessert, which is usually brought after the other dishes have been removed.

A Feast for All the Senses

The ideal Thai meal aims at being a harmonious blend of the spicy, the sweet and the sour, and is meant to be satisfying to the eyes, nose and palate. Sometimes several of these flavors are subtly blended in a single dish, while sometimes one predominates. In addition to the rice, a typical meal might also include a soup, a curry or two, a salad, a fried and a steamed dish.

There will also be a variety of sauces and condiments: *nam pla*, the indispensable Thai fish sauce—a salt substitute made from fermented fish; *nam prik*, which is a spicier version of *nam pla* mixed with chopped chilies and other ingredients; crushed dried chilies in addition to fresh ones

like bird's-eye chilies for those who like their food really hot; pickled garlic; locally made chili sauce, and such fresh vegetables as cucumbers, tomatoes, long beans, water spinach and spring onions.

The most common dessert is one or more of the delectable fruits that are so abundant in Thailand, such as mangoes, jackfruit, lychees, and rambutans. On special occasions, more elaborate desserts may be served, such as Foi Thong ("golden threads"); Sangkaya Fak Thong, a decorative pumpkin custard; and Tab Tim Grob ("red rubies"), water chestnut pieces in a red coating of tapioca flour served in sweet coconut cream and shaved ice.

OPPOSITE: Indispensable wire-mesh baskets used for deep-frying and set of bamboo trays useful for steaming over a wok.
BELOW: A late 19th century mural shows the traditional way of eating with the hand while seated on the floor.

Authentic Thai Ingredients

Dried red chilies

Bird's-eye chilies

Fresh red chilies

Bamboo shoots or *naw mai* are the fresh shoots of bamboo, and make an excellent vegetable. They must first be peeled, sliced and simmered for about 30 minutes until tender. If using canned bamboo shoots, remove any metallic taste by draining the shoots then boiling them in fresh water for 5 minutes.

Bean curd or *tofu* is available in various forms and consistencies. Soft and firm white bean curd is often steamed or added to soups. Small squares of **pressed bean curd** are used in place of meat in stir-fries or spring rolls. Cubes of **deep-fried bean curd**, also known as *tau hoo tod*, are added to slow-cooked dishes

and some soups. Pickled or **fermented bean curd**, known as *tau hoo yee*, sold in jars and either red or light brown in color, is used in small amounts as a seasoning in Chinese-influenced dishes.

Bean sprouts, also known as sprouted mung beans or *tau ngork*, are eaten raw or lightly blanched in salads and soups, or quickly stir-fried as a vegetable dish. They can be stored in a refrigerator for 2–3 days.

Cardamom or *luk grawan* are straw-colored pods containing 8–10 tiny black seeds that have an intense fragrance. They are used in southern Thai curries.

Chilies are indispensable in Thai cooking and many different varieties are used. The large, finger-length green, red or yellow chili (*prik chee*) is moderately hot. **Dried red chilies** of this variety are ground to make chili flakes or ground red pepper. Tiny red, green or yellowy-orange **bird's-eye chilies** (*prik kee noo*) are used in soups, curries and sauces, and are extremely hot. They are also available dried.

Chili sauce or *saus prik* is made by mixing chilies with water and seasoning the mixture with salt, sugar and vinegar or lime juice. It is available bottled and in jars; the best known brand overseas is *Siracha*. Some sauces are sweeter than others, and go particularly well with either chicken or seafood (and are so labeled).

Thai basil (*horapa*)   Lemon basil (*manglak*)   Holy basil (*kaprow*)

Basil is often used as a seasoning and garnish in Thai cooking, and there are several types. The most commonly used basil is known as **Thai basil** or *horapa* and is fairly similar to European and American sweet basil. It is used liberally as a seasoning and sprigs of it are often added to platters of fresh raw vegetables. **Lemon basil** or *manglak* is similar to *horapa* but paler and with a distinctive lemony fragrance. It is used in soups and salads. *Kaprow*, sometimes known as "holy basil," has a fragrance redolent of cloves. Its taste is sharp and hot and it is mainly used in spicy stir-fries. Thai basils are commonly available in Asian food stores and many supermarkets, but sweet basil makes an acceptable substitute.

Chinese celery or *ceun chai* is much smaller with thinner stems than the normal Western variety, and has a very intense, parsley-like flavor. The leaves and sometimes the stems are added to soups, rice dishes and stir-fried vegetables. This type of celery is obtainable in Asian speciality stores.

Chinese garlic chives or *kui chai* have a far more emphatic, garlicky flavor than Western chives and resemble flat spring onions.

Coriander leaves, also known as cilantro or Chinese parsley, are very widely used in Thai cooking. In fact, the Thais use all parts of the coriander plant. The flavor of the leaves enhances countless dishes. Coriander roots are pounded together with garlic and black pepper to provide a basic seasoning for soups and stir-fries. Dried coriander seeds are used to season curries. There is no substitute for fresh coriander; it can easily be grown from the seeds and is now available in most supermarkets, sold in bunches with the roots still attached.

Coconut cream and **coconut milk** are used in many Thai desserts and curries. To obtain fresh coconut cream (which is normally used for desserts), grate the flesh of 1 coconut into a bowl (this yields about 3 cups of grated coconut flesh), add $1/2$ cup water and knead thoroughly a few times, then squeeze the mixture firmly in your fist or strain with a muslin cloth or cheese cloth. **Thick coconut milk** is obtained by the same method but by adding double the water to the grated flesh (about 1

cup instead of $1/2$ cup). **Thin coconut milk** (which is used for curries rather than desserts) is obtained by pressing the coconut a second time, adding 1 cup of water to the same grated coconut flesh and squeezing it again. Although freshly pressed milk has more flavor, coconut cream and milk are now widely sold canned or in packets that are quick, convenient and quite tasty. Canned or packet coconut cream or milk comes in varying consistencies depending on the brand, and you will need to try them out and adjust the thickness by adding water as needed. In general, you should add 1 cup of water to 1 cup of canned or packet coconut cream to obtain thick coconut milk, and 2 cups of water to 1 cup of coconut cream to obtain thin coconut milk. These mixing ratios are only general guides, however, and you can adjust the thickness depending on individual taste.

Cumin or *mellet yira* is often added to curry pastes. The same Thai name is used for cumin, fennel and caraway, which are all similar in appearance, sometimes leading to confusion.

Dried prawns or **dried shrimp** (*kung haeng*) are used to season many dishes, particularly sauces. They can be small or large; the better quality ones are bright orange in color and shelled. They should first be soaked in warm water for 5 minutes to soften.

Fish sauce or *nam pla* is indispensable in Thai cooking. Made from salted, fermented fish or prawns, good quality *nam pla* is golden-brown in color and has a salty tang. It is used in the same way as the Chinese use soy sauce. It is sold in bottles and is available in most supermarkets.

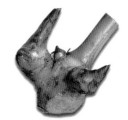

Galangal or *kha* is a rhizome, similar to ginger in appearance and a member of the same family. It adds a distinctive fragrance and flavor to many

Thai dishes. Slices of dried galangal (sometimes sold under the Indonesian name *laos* or the Malaysian name *lengkuas*) must be soaked in hot water for about 30 minutes to soften before using. But dried galangal lacks the fragrance of fresh galangal, and most Asian food stores sell it fresh. It can be sliced and kept sealed in the freezer for several months.

Ginger or *king* is one of the most common ingredients in Asian cooking. Use only fresh ginger in Thai cooking; dried powdered ginger has a completely different flavor. Young ginger, which is pale yellow with a pinkish tinge, is juicier than mature ginger, which has a brown skin that should be scraped off before use.

Jicama or *mun kaew* (also known as *bangkuang* or yam bean) is a crunchy, mild tuber with a white interior and beige skin which peels off easily. It is excellent eaten raw with a spicy dip, and can also be cooked. Daikon radish may be used as a substitute.

Kaffir lime or *ma-grood* is a small lime that has a very knobby and intensely fragrant skin, but virtually no juice. The skin or rind is often grated and added to dishes as a seasoning. The fragrant leaves are added whole to soups and curries, or finely shredded and added to salads or deep-fried fish cakes, giving a wonderfully tangy taste to these dishes. They are available frozen or dried in Asian food stores; frozen leaves are more flavorful. The dried rind can be reconstituted and substituted for fresh.

Krachai, also known as Chinese keys or lesser ginger, is an unusual rhizome which looks like a bunch of yellowish-brown fingers, and is enjoyed for its mild flavor and crunchy texture. It gives a subtle spicy flavor to dishes. Dried *krachai* is a poor substitute, so if the fresh variety is not available, omit this.

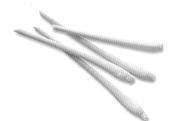

Lemongrass or *bai takrai* (also known as citronella) is a lemon-scented stem which grows in clumps, and is very important in Thai cooking. Each plant resembles a miniature leek. Use only the thicker bottom one third of the lemongrass stem. Discard the dry outer leaves and use only the tender inner part of the plant. Lemongrass is available fresh, frozen or dried; fresh lemongrass is preferable because of its stronger smell and flavor.

Dried Chinese mushrooms

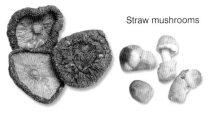

Straw mushrooms

Mushrooms are prized in Thai cooking for the flavor and texture they add to dishes. Fresh mushrooms of several varieties are used, including delicate sheathed **straw mushrooms**

(excellent in soups and vegetable dishes); **button mushrooms**; and dried brownish-black **Chinese mushrooms** (similar to Japanese shiitake mushrooms, which may also be used) which should be soaked in warm water to soften before use.

Oyster mushrooms are fan-shaped mushrooms that are usually white or grayish-brown in color. They grow in clusters and are sometimes known as abalone mushrooms.

Oyster sauce, also known as *nam man hoi,* is often used in conjunction with fish sauce or soy sauce. Most brands of oyster sauce contain monosodium glutamate and therefore intensify the flavor of the dish to which they are added. Mushroom sauce or a combination of fish sauce and soy sauce is a good substitute.

Palm sugar or *nam taan peep* is made from the distilled juice of various palm fruits (especially the coconut and arenga palms). Palm sugar varies in color from gold to dark brown. It has a rich flavor similar to dark brown sugar, molasses or maple syrup, which make good substitues.

Pandanus leaves or *bai toey hom* come from a member of the pandanus palm or screwpine family. Pandanus leaves are used as a wrapping for seasoned morsels of chicken or pork rib. Look for fresh leaves at

Fresh egg noodles

Kwaytiaow

Rice vermicelli

Glass noodles

Noodles are available in many forms, and are made from either rice, wheat or mung bean flour. Kwaytiaow, also known as *hofun*, are wide, flat rice-flour noodles sold fresh in Asian markets. If fresh *kwaytiaow* cannot be obtained, use dried **rice-stick noodles** instead (these are thinner than *kwaytiaow* and must be soaked in hot water for 5 minutes and drained before use). **Dried rice vermicelli** are very fine rice threads that must also be soaked before using. **Kanom jeen** are spaghetti-like rice-flour noodles which are similar to the *laksa* noodles of Malaysia and Singapore. **Egg noodles** (*ba mee*) are made from wheat flour. **Glass noodles**, also known as cellophane noodles or bean threads, are thin transparent noodles made from mung bean flour. They are sold in dried form and must be soaked in warm water briefly to soften.

Southeast Asian produce stands. One-ounce packages of dried leaves labeled "Dried Bay-Tovy Leaves" are imported from Thailand, but fresh leaves are preferred.

Rice flour made from ground long grain rice is used to make dough and batter, mainly for Thai desserts. Fresh rice flour was traditionally made by soaking rice overnight and grinding it slowly in a stone mill. The same result may be achieved by grinding soaked rice in a blender. Dried rice flour is available in some Asian specialty shops, as is **glutinous rice flour** made from sticky glutinous rice.

Salted cabbage or *pak kad khem* is used in some Thai-Chinese dishes. Soak in fresh water for at least 15 minutes to remove excess saltiness, repeating if necessary.

Salted duck eggs or *kai khem* are used as a side dish or pounded to make a sauce. The eggs should be boiled for about 10 minutes before being peeled.

Salted soy beans or *tau jiew* are slightly fermented and have a distinctive tang. These are often lightly pounded before being used to season fish, noodles or some vegetable dishes. Varieties packed in China are sometimes confusingly labeled "Yellow Bean Sauce," while there are also brands which add sugar or chili to already ground beans. Japanese *miso* is similar and may be substituted.

Salted fish or *pla haeng* is prepared by cleaning and salting freshly-caught fish that are splayed open on racks and dried in the sun. Many varieties of fish are used. They are either grilled or cut into fine slices and fried to a crisp, then added to other ingredients and ground to make dipping sauces.

Shrimp paste or *kapi* is a dense mixture of fermented ground shrimp. It is sold in dried blocks and ranges in color from pink to blackish-brown. Shrimp paste should be cooked before eating to kill bacteria; if the recipe you are using does not call for it to be fried together with other ingredients later, first either grill or dry-fry the shrimp paste before adding to other ingredients.

Soy sauce or *nam siew* is often used in dishes of Chinese origin. Regular Chinese light soy sauce and the darker black soy sauce are both used in this book. Light soy is saltier, while black soy adds a richer flavor and color to cooked dishes.

Tamarind or *mak-kaam* is a sour fruit that comes in a hard pod shell. Mix 3 tablespoons dried tamarind pulp with $1/2$ cup warm water, then mash well and strain through a sieve to obtain sour, fragrant tamarind juice. Discard any seeds and fibrous matter. If using already cleaned tamarind pulp or concentrate, reduce the amounts called for in these recipes.

Turmeric or *kamin* is a member of the ginger family. This rhizome has a very rich yellow interior (which can stain clothing and plastic utensils) and a pleasant pungency that is absent in dried turmeric powder. Substitute $1/2$ teaspoon turmeric powder for $1/2$ inch fresh turmeric.

Vinegar is commonly used in Thai recipes. Usually distilled white vinegar or Chinese black vinegar is used. It is often used to make condiments or as a preservative and any sort of vinegar may be substituted.

Water chestnuts or *haew* are crunchy, white and juicy-sweet inside. The dark brown skin should be peeled before eating, and it is well worth using fresh water chestnuts if you can find them. Their crisp texture and sweet flavor make them popular in salads, stir-fried vegetable dishes and desserts.

Water spinach or *pak bung* is also known in Thailand as morning glory (and as *kangkung* in Indonesia, Malaysia and Singapore). This aquatic plant is a delicious and nutritious vegetable. Young shoots are often served as part of a mixed platter of raw vegetables for dipping into hot sauces, while the leaves and tender tips are also stir-fried. Discard the tough, hollow stems.

Authentic Thai Recipes

Portions
In Thai homes, food is seldom served in individual portions, as main dishes and condiments are normally placed on the table for people to help themselves, family style. Small amounts of these dishes are eaten with copious amounts of fragrant fluffy rice or sticky glutinous rice. It is thus difficult to estimate the exact number of portions each recipe will provide. As a general rule, however, the recipes in this book will serve 4–6 people as part of a meal with rice and three other main dishes.

Thai seasonings
Thais are fond of strong flavors—fiery chilies, salty fish sauce, soothing coconut, sweet palm sugar, and sour tamarind or lime. The amounts of chili, fish sauce, sugar and lime juice given in the following recipes is a guide, not an absolute measure. Bear in mind that you can always increase or decrease the amount of seasonings when preparing a dish, and condiments at the table may be added individually, so be careful not to overdo it in the initial stages.

Curry pastes
Basic curry pastes (recipes start on the next page) can be prepared in large quantities and stored in a covered glass jar in a refrigerator for 1 month or in a freezer for 3–4 months.

Ingredients
When a recipe lists a hard-to-find or unusual ingredient, see pages 18–21 for possible substitutes. If a substitute is not listed, look for the ingredient in your local Asian food market. Many Thai ingredients are now available in supermarkets outside of Thailand—including coriander leaf (cilantro), galangal root, fish sauce, coconut cream, palm sugar and lemon grass. Look for ingredients that are more difficult to find in Asian specialty shops. You can also check the Internet listings on page 112 for possible sources.

Time estimates
Estimates are given for preparation and cooking, and are based on the assumption that a food processor or blender will be used to grind spices.

Tips on grinding spices
When using a mortar and pestle or blender when preparing curry pastes, slice or chop the ingredients first before grinding. Also grind the tougher ingredients first before you add the softer ones. Add a little liquid (oil, coconut milk or water, depending on the recipe) to keep the blades turning. Be sure not to overload the blender—divide the ingredients into batches and grind each batch before adding the next. If you have to roast some ingredients before grinding, cool them a bit before adding to the blender. Store unused spice pastes in an airtight container in the freezer.

Thai Chicken Stock
Nam Cheua Gai

5–6 1/2 lbs (2 1/2–3 kg) chicken bones
  or 1/2 whole chicken
6 quarts (liters) water
1 1/2 cups (250 g) chopped onion
1 cup (125 g) chopped celery
1 tablespoon coriander seeds
1 teaspoon black peppercorns

Wash bones in cold water then put in a stockpot and cover with cold water. Bring rapidly to the boil, then drain and discard water. Cover bones with 6 quarts water and add all other ingredients. Simmer for 3 hours, removing the scum as it accumulates. Strain through cloth. The stock can be put in 1-quart containers and frozen for up to 3 months. Home made chicken stock greatly improves the flavor of all recipes where stock is specified. Yields 2 liters of stock.

Preparation time: 15 mins
Cooking time: 3 hours

Green Chili Sauce
Nam Jim

3 cloves garlic, crushed
3 large green chilies, slit open, seeded and chopped
3 coriander roots, scraped clean
3 shallots, chopped
5–6 bird's-eye chilies (optional)
2–3 tablespoons shaved palm
  sugar
2–3 tablespoons lime juice
2 tablespoons fish sauce

Grind the garlic, green chilies, coriander roots, shallots and bird's-eye chilies, if using, in a mortar and pestle or blender. Add the palm sugar, lime juice and fish sauce, and mix well. This sauce is usually eaten with grilled seafood. Yields 3/4 cup.

Preparation time: 5 mins

Prawn Chili Paste
Nam Prik Pow

1/2 cup (125 ml) vegetable oil
8 shallots, sliced
6 cloves garlic, sliced
1 cup (100 g) dried prawns or shrimp
1/2 cup (30 g) dried chilies, cut roughly
1 tablespoon palm sugar
3 tablespoons fish sauce
2 1/2 tablespoons tamarind juice (page 21)

Heat the oil in a wok and fry the shallots and garlic until golden brown; remove from oil and set aside. Add the dried prawns and chilies and fry until golden brown; remove from oil and set aside. In a food processor or blender, process the shallots, garlic, prawns, chilies and sugar with a little cooled oil from the wok to keep the blades turning. Add the fish sauce, tamarind juice and salt and blend to obtain about 1 3/4 cups of paste.

Preparation time: 5 mins
Cooking time: 15 mins

Red Curry Paste
Nam Prik Gaeng Ped

1 tablespoon coriander seeds
1 teaspoon cumin seed
5 dried red chilies, slit lengthwise, deseeded and soaked in hot water for 15 minutes
3 tablespoons sliced shallots
8 cloves garlic, smashed
2–3 thin slices galangal
2 tablespoons sliced lemongrass (inside of thickest part of stem only)
2 teaspoons grated kaffir lime rind
1 tablespoon chopped coriander root
10 black peppercorns
1 teaspoon dried shrimp paste

Dry-fry the coriander and cumin seeds in a wok or frying pan over low heat for about 5 minutes, then grind to a powder in a blender or mortar and pestle. Add the remaining ingredients, except the shrimp paste, and grind well. Add the shrimp paste and grind again to obtain about 3/4 cup (180 ml) of fine-textured curry paste.

Preparation time: 15 mins
Cooking time: 5 mins

Green Curry Paste
Nam Prik Gaeng Kheow Wan

1 tablespoon coriander seeds
1 teaspoon cumin seeds
5–10 green bird's-eye chilies
3 tablespoons sliced shallots
3 cloves garlic, sliced
1 teaspoon sliced galangal
1 tablespoon sliced lemongrass (inside of thickest part of stem only)
1/2 teaspoon grated kaffir lime rind
1 teaspoon chopped coriander root
5 black peppercorns
1 teaspoon salt
1 teaspoon dried shrimp paste, roasted (page 21)

Dry-fry the coriander and cumin seeds in a wok over low heat for about 5 minutes, then grind to a powder. Add the rest of the ingredients, except the shrimp paste, and grind to mix well. Add the shrimp paste to the spice mixture and grind to obtain 1/2 cup of fine-textured curry paste.

Preparation time: 15 mins
Cooking time: 5 mins

Mussaman Curry Paste
Nam Prik Gaeng Mussaman

3 tablespoons sliced shallots
1 tablespoon chopped garlic
1 teaspoon sliced galangal
1 heaped tablespoon sliced lemongrass (inside of thickest part of stem only)
2 cloves
1 tablespoon coriander seeds
1 teaspoon cumin seeds
5 black peppercorns
3 dried chilies, sliced open, deseeded and soaked in hot water for 15 minutes
1 teaspoon salt
1 teaspoon dried shrimp paste

Dry-fry the shallots, garlic, galangal, lemongrass, cloves, coriander and cumin seeds in a wok over low heat for about 5 minutes, then grind to a powder in a mortar and pestle or blender. Add the rest of the ingredients, except the shrimp paste, and grind to mix well. Combine the ground mixture and shrimp paste and grind again to obtain 1/2 cup of fine-textured curry paste.

Preparation time: 5 mins
Cooking time: 15 mins

Sweet and Sour Chili Sauce

3 shallots, thinly sliced
1/2 teaspoon dried chili flakes or ground red pepper
2 tablespoons fish sauce
2 tablespoons lime juice
2 tablespoons sugar
1 tablespoon water

Place the ingredients in a small saucepan and bring to a boil over medium heat. Reduce heat to low and simmer for 5 minutes, until sauce begins to thicken. Remove from heat and serve as a dipping sauce for roast pork or chicken

Preparation time: 5 mins
Cooking time: 10 mins

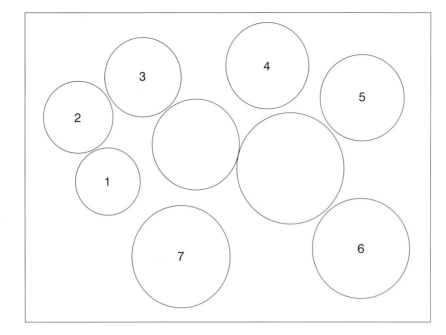

Key to photograph appearing on pages 24–25: A traditional northern Thai appetizer platter consisting of various raw vegetables, fried fish and chicken wings, and dipping sauces.

1   Salted Fish and Coconut Dip
2   Pork and Prawn Coconut Dip
3   Spicy Grilled Fish Dip
4   Green Peppercorn Prawn Dip
5   Shrimp Paste and Chili Dip
6   Green Chili and Salted Fish Dip
7   Spicy Salted Egg Dip

Salted Fish and Coconut Dip   Kapi Kua

2 dried chilies, cut open, deseeded and soaked
5 shallots, sliced
3 stems lemongrass (inside of thickest part of stem only), finely sliced
3 slices galangal
1 teaspoon minced *krachai* (page 20)
3 tablespoons dried shrimp paste, roasted
$1/2$ cup (90 g) salted fish, soaked in water for 15 minutes and coarsely chopped
4 cups (1 liter) coconut milk
$1/2$ tablespoon palm sugar
$1/2$ tablespoon fish sauce
1–3 red chilies

Grind together the dried chilies, shallots, lemongrass, galangal, *krachai* and shrimp paste with half the fish until well mixed. Heat the coconut milk and simmer until oil comes to the surface and the quantity has reduced. Add the paste and continue cooking until fragrant. Add the rest of the fish, sugar, fish sauce and chilies and cook over low heat, stirring frequently, until the sauce has thickened and reduced. Yields $1^1/4$ cup.

Preparation time: 25 mins
Cooking time: 15 mins

Pork and Prawn Coconut Dip   Tau Jiew Lon

1 cup (250 ml) coconut cream
$1/2$ cup water
3 shallots, sliced
3 tablespoons salted fermented soy beans (*tau jiew*), mashed
5 fresh prawns (about 2 oz/70 g), shelled, deveined and chopped
2 oz (60 g) minced pork
$1/2$ tablespoon palm sugar
1 egg (optional), beaten
3 red chilies, chopped (or 1–2 teaspoons dried chili flakes)
Fresh coriander leaves (cilantro)

Add coconut cream to water and bring to a boil. Add shallots, salted soy beans, shrimp, pork and palm sugar. Mix well and stir in egg, if using, stirring constantly. Cook until slightly reduced, then add chili shreds and garnish with coriander leaf. Yields $2^1/2$ cups.

Preparation time: 5 mins
Cooking time: 25 miins

Spicy Grilled Fish Dip   Nam Prik Pla Yaang

3–4 bird's-eye chilies
1 dried chili, cut open, deseeded and soaked
3 cloves garlic, grilled in skin until blackened, then peeled
2 shallots, grilled in skin until blackened, then peeled
$1/2$ teaspoon dried shrimp paste, roasted (page 21)
2 tablespoons (30 g) cooked or fried fish, flaked
2 tablespoons lime juice
1 tablespoon fish sauce
1 teaspoon sugar
1 kaffir lime leaf, thinly sliced

Grind together bird's-eye chilies, dried chili, garlic, shallots and shrimp paste. Add flaked fish, lime juice, fish sauce, sugar and sliced kaffir lime leaf. Mix well to obtain $3/4$ cup of dip. Serve with vegetables and grilled or fried fish.

Preparation time: 10 mins
Cooking time: 10 mins

Green Peppercorn Prawn Dip Nam Prik Thai Orn

2 tablespoons green peppercorns
3 cloves garlic, sliced
1 teaspoon sugar
1/2 tablespoon dried prawns, soaked in warm water for 10 minutes and drained
2–3 tablespoons lime juice
6 sour fruits such as green mango or green apple, sliced

If using bottled or canned green peppercorns, wash off brine thoroughly first. Grind together the garlic and 1 tablespoon of peppercorns. Add sugar, dried prawns, lime juice and the remaining tablespoon of peppercorns and grind to yield 1 cup of dip. Serve with sour fruit, vegetables and fried or grilled fish.

Preparation time: 15 mins

Shrimp Paste and Chili Dip Nam Prik Kapi

1 tablespoon dried prawns or shrimp, soaked in warm water for 10 minutes and drained
5 cloves garlic, sliced
4–6 bird's-eye chilies
1 tablespoon dried shrimp paste, roasted (page 21)
1 teaspoon shaved palm sugar
1 teaspoon fish sauce
2–3 tablespoons lime juice

Grind dried shrimp, garlic and chilies together. Add shrimp paste, palm sugar, fish sauce and lime juice and mix well to obtain 1/4 cup of dip. Serve with raw or cooked vegetables and fried or grilled fish.

Preparation time: 15 mins

Green Chili and Salted Fish Dip Nam Prik Noom

1 tablespoon dried salted fish, soaked in warm water for 10 minutes, drained and chopped
4 tablespoons oil
5–10 green chilies, chopped
10 cloves garlic, chopped
6 shallots, chopped
1 ripe tomato, sliced
2 tablespoons hot water
1 tablespoon chopped spring onion
1 tablespoon chopped coriander leaves (cilantro)
1 teaspoon fish sauce, or to taste

Fry the salted fish in the oil over medium heat for about 7–10 minutes and drain thoroughly. Dry-fry the chilies, garlic and shallots for about 8–10 minutes, stirring frequently, until fragrant. Pound lightly or blend briefly with the fish, then add the tomato. Pound or blend to break up the tomato, then add water, spring onion and coriander leaf. Mix well to obtain 1 cup of dip. The sauce should be of a reasonably liquid consistency and a touch salty; if not, add more water or fish sauce as required. This very hot dip is traditionally served with sticky rice as well as raw cabbage, sliced cucumbers, raw green beans and/or fried or roasted fish.

Preparation time: 5 mins
Cooking time: 20 mins

Pork and Tomato Chili Dip Nam Prik Ong

5 dried chilies, cut open, deseeded and soaked in hot water for 10 minutes
1 teaspoon salt
1 tablespoon sliced galangal
3 tablespoons chopped onion
1 teaspoon dried shrimp paste, roasted (page 21)
5 cloves garlic
3 oz (75 g) ground pork
1 cup (170 g) ripe tomatoes, diced
2 tablespoons oil
3 cloves garlic, chopped

1/2 cup (125 ml) water
1 sprig coriander leaf (cilantro), chopped
Raw vegetables: cucumber, long beans, carrot, cabbage
Steamed vegetables: long beans, eggplant (aubergine), pumpkin, cabbage

Grind the chilies, salt and galangal in a mortar and pestle or blender. Add the onion, shrimp paste and garlic cloves and grind thoroughly. Add the pork and continue processing. Add the tomatoes and mix. Heat oil in a wok, then fry the chopped garlic until fragrant. Add ground mixture and continue frying over low heat, stirring, until the ingredients take on a gloss. Add the water and continue cooking, stirring until much of the water evaporates and the mixture becomes fairly thick. Transfer to a bowl, then sprinkle with chopped cilantro. Serve with fresh vegetables or boiled vegetables or both. Yields 1 cup.

Preparation time: 25 mins
Cooking time: 30 mins

Spicy Salted Egg Dip Nam Prik Gai Kem

3 cloves garlic, sliced
3–4 red chilies, sliced
2 salted eggs, shelled
2 tablespoons lime juice
1/2 tablespoon fish sauce
1 teaspoon sugar

Grind garlic and chilies together in a blender or mortar and pestle. Add salted eggs and grind until well blended. Season with lime juice, fish sauce and sugar. Mix well to obtain 1/2 cup of dip. Serve with raw vegetables and fried or grilled fish.

Preparation time: 20 mins

Leaf-wrapped Savory Morsels Mieng Kum

This is a snack or appetizer eaten at home, rather than at streetside stalls or in restaurants, and goes very well with beer or cocktails. In Thailand, various edible tree leaves are used to wrap the fillings, but soft lettuce leaves like butter lettuce or red lettuce make a fine substitute. The point is to wrap a selection of flavorful tidbits in a lettuce leaf with a touch of sauce and pop the whole packet in your mouth.

1 small head of lettuce (preferably a soft-leaf lettuce like butter or red leaf)
5 tablespoons freshly grated coconut or unsweetened dried coconut, roasted in moderate oven or dry-fried in wok or frying pan until light brown, 1–3 minutes
3 tablespoons diced shallots
3 tablespoons diced lime (if thin-rind calamansi or young limes are available, leave rind on)
3 tablespoons diced fresh ginger root or galangal root (or both)
3 tablespoons dried prawns or shrimp, soaked in warm water for 5 minutes, drained and chopped
3 tablespoons unsalted roasted peanuts, whole or crushed
2 tablespoons chopped or whole chilies
Handful of leafy herbs like shiso, mint, basil, coriander leaves (cilantro) or pepper leaves

Sauce
1 tablespoon dried shrimp paste
$1/2$ tablespoon sliced galangal
$1/2$ tablespoon sliced shallots
2 tablespoons grated fresh coconut
3 tablespoons chopped unsalted peanuts
2 tablespoons chopped dried shrimp, soaked in warm water for 10 minutes and drained
1 teaspoon sliced fresh ginger
1 cup (150 g) chopped or shaved palm sugar
$2^1/2$ cups (625 ml) water

1 Prepare the Sauce first. Dry roast the shrimp paste, galangal and shallots in a frying pan or under a broiler until fragrant, then leave to cool. Place in a blender, food processor or mortar and pestle with the coconut, peanuts, shrimp and ginger, and grind until fine.
2 Transfer the mixture into a heavy-bottomed pan with the sugar and water, mix well and bring to a boil. Simmer until it is reduced to about 1 cup, then let it cool.
3 To serve, pour the Sauce into a serving bowl and arrange all the ingredients in separate piles on small bowls.
4 To eat, take a lettuce leaf, place a small amount of each of the filling ingredients in the middle, top with a dollop of sauce and bits of herbs and fold up into a little package.

Serves 4   Preparation time: 15 mins   Cooking time: 30 mins

Eggs with Tangy Tamarind Dressing
Kai Look Kuay

The sweet-sour-salty combination of tamarind juice, fish sauce and sugar in the sauce is what makes this a divine starter or main dish. Try using dark brown sugar, palm sugar or maple syrup and adding a touch of fresh chili for an even more interesting combination—and adjust the tamarind, fish sauce and sugar to your personal taste.

4 cups (1 liter) water
6 eggs
2 cups (500 ml) oil
Coriander leaves (cilantro) to garnish

Tamarind Dressing
5 tablespoons tamarind pulp mixed with $^1/_2$ cup (125 ml) water, mashed and
    strained to remove seeds and fibers
2 tablespoons fish sauce
$^1/_2$ cup (100 g) sugar

Crispy-fried Shallots
$^1/_4$ cup (60 ml) oil
$^1/_2$ cup thinly sliced shallots

1 To prepare the Crispy-fried Shallots, heat the oil in a wok over medium heat. Add the shallots and stir-fry for 5 minutes or until shallots begin to turn golden brown. Do not overcook. Quickly remove the shallots from the wok with a slotted spoon, drain on a paper towel and set aside.
2 To make the Tamarind Dressing, combine all the ingredients in a pan, bring to the boil and simmer for 5 minutes until it begins to thicken, stirring well to dissolve the sugar. Set aside.
3 Pour the water into a pot, bring to the boil then boil the eggs for 5 minutes. Remove the eggs from the water with a ladle and plunge into cold water. When eggs are cool, peel off the shells and set aside.
4 Heat the oil in a wok or saucepan over medium heat. Dry the eggs and deep-fry until they turn golden brown on the outside, about 3–4 minutes. Drain and set aside to cool.
5 Slice the eggs in half lengthwise, pour the sauce over the eggs and serve garnished with Crispy-fried Shallots and coriander leaves (cilantro).

Serves 4–6   Preparation time: 5 mins   Cooking time: 8 mins

Pork and Shrimp Bean Curd Skin Dumplings   Tong Geon Yong

The Chinese influence on this dish is evident in the use of dried bean curd skin as the wrapping. The filling can be made in advance and the dumplings assembled just before frying, so they may be served piping hot.

3–4 coriander stems and roots
3 cloves garlic
1/2 teaspoon white peppercorns
4 oz (125 g) fresh shrimp or prawns, peeled and deveined, finely minced
4 oz (125 g) ground pork
1 teaspoon soy sauce
4–6 sheets of dried bean curd skin (available in Asian food markets)
4 cups (1 liter) oil for deep-frying

1 Grind the coriander roots, garlic and peppercorn in a mortar and pestle or spice grinder until they form a paste. Combine the paste with the shrimp, pork and soy sauce.
2 Wipe sheets of dried bean curd skin with a moist cloth to soften and cut into 4 x 6 in (10 x 15 cm) squares. Place a tablespoon of the filling on each square and roll it up like a cigar. Alternatively, cut circles about 4 1/2 in (11 cm) in diameter and place a little filling in the center of each. Squeeze in the sides to make a bundle and tie with a strip of spring onion or garlic chive (as shown in the photo).
3 Deep-fry the rolls in hot oil over medium-high heat until golden brown. Serve with soy sauce or sweet chili sauce.

Makes 14 dumplings   Preparation time: 20 mins   Cooking time: 15 mins

Crispy Shells with Minced Chicken   Krathong Thong

The delicate crisp shells used for this snack are made using a special *krathong* brass mold. Thin short-crust pastry shells or *vol-au-vent* cases can be used instead.

Shells
1/2 cup (80 g) rice flour
6 tablespoons all-purpose (plain) flour
4 tablespoons thin coconut milk
2 tablespoons tapioca starch (tapioca flour) or cornstarch
1 egg yolk
1/4 teaspoon sugar
1/4 teaspoon salt
1/4 teaspoon baking soda (bicarbonate of soda)
4 cups (1 liter) oil for deep-frying

Filling
1 tablespoon oil
4 tablespoons finely diced onion
7 oz (200 g) ground chicken or pork
1/4 cup (60 ml) fresh or canned corn kernels (sweetcorn)
2 tablespoons finely diced carrot
1/2 tablespoon sugar
1/4 teaspoon black soy sauce
1/2 teaspoon salt
1/2 teaspoon white pepper
Coriander leaves (cilantro) for garnish
1 red chili, finely sliced

1 Make the Shells first by mixing all ingredients, except oil, together in a bowl. Heat the oil in a wok, then dip the *krathong* mold in the oil to heat up. Dip the mold into the batter and plunge back into oil. Fry for about 5 minutes until light brown, then shake to remove the cup from the mold. Place on paper towels to drain. Repeat until all the batter is used up.
2 Now make the Filling. Put the oil in a hot wok and stir-fry onion and chicken or pork until browned, about 2 minutes. Add the rest of the ingredients and fry for about 3 minutes until the vegetables are fairly soft. Leave them to cool, then divide the filling among the Shells.
3 Garnish with coriander leaves (cilantro) and slices of fresh red chili.

Note: If you cannot obtain rice flour, you can make your own by first soaking 1/2 cup long grain rice in water for 5 hours. Drain and transfer the rice to a blender. Add 1/2 cup water and grind till a thick liquid mixture forms. Pour the mixture into a fine sieve and leave until the water drains and a paste forms. Dry the paste in the sun until completely dry. When completely dry, crumble it and sieve it to obtain the rice flour.
If using a *krathong* mold, be sure that it is very hot before plunging it into the batter; the batter must adhere to the mold when you put it back into the oil to cook.

Makes 20–25 pieces   Preparation time: 15 mins   Cooking time: 30 mins

Savory Stuffed Omelets Kai Yad Sai

Frequently found on the menu of simple restaurants as well as at roadside stalls, this is often eaten at lunch time with rice and makes a satisfying meal with one other vegetable dish.

1/4 cup (60 ml) oil
6 oz (150 g) ground pork or chicken
3 tablespoons diced cherry tomatoes
3 tablespoons fresh or frozen green
   peas
2 tablespoons minced onion
2 teaspoons sugar
1 1/2 tablespoons fish sauce
1/4 teaspoon black soy sauce
1/4 teaspoon ground white pepper
3 eggs, beaten
2 sprigs coriander leaves (cilantro),
   to garnish
1 finely sliced red chili, to garnish

1 Heat half of the oil in a wok over high heat and stir-fry the meat for 2 minutes or until cooked. Add the tomatoes, green peas, onion, sugar, fish sauce, soy sauce and pepper. Stir-fry another 2–3 minutes until cooked then set aside.

2 Heat a small skillet or omelet pan 6–8 in (12–20 cm) in diameter and add a drop of the remaining oil. Pour in enough egg to thinly cover the base. Brown the omelet lightly on both sides, being careful to turn the omelet over gently halfway through cooking.

3 To stuff the omelet, place 1–2 spoonfuls of the meat mixture in the center, fold two opposite sides toward the center and then fold in the remaining sides so that the omelet forms a square. Place on a serving plate and repeat until all the egg and pork mixture is used up.

4 Garnish with coriander leaves (cilantro) and finely sliced red chili. Serve accompanied by rice.

Note: To present omelets as shown in the photo on the opposite page, turn each omelet over so the folded edges are face down. Make a cross-shaped slit in the top of each omelet and then fold the slit portions back.

Serves 4   Preparation time: 15 mins   Cooking time: 10 mins

Heat half of the oil in the wok and stir-fry the pork mixture.

Place 1–2 spoonfuls of the pork mixture in the center of each omelet.

Fold two opposite sides of each omelet toward the center.

Steamed Seafood Cakes Haw Mok Thalay

A universally popular dish well worth the time needed to prepare it, this mixture of seafood, coconut milk and seasonings is steamed in small cups made of banana leaf. It is possible to use aluminium foil or small cup-cake tins or small heatproof bowls instead. Rather than a number of small cakes, you can also make one large cake about 1 in (3 cm) thick, in an 8 x 8 in (20 x 20 cm) heatproof cake or brownie dish, and then slice it into squares for serving.

$^3/_4$ cup (180 ml) coconut cream
1 teaspoon rice flour
4 oz (100 g) boneless white fish fillets, cut into thin slices
4 oz (100 g) fresh shrimp or prawns, peeled and deveined, cut into small pieces
4 oz (100 g) squid, cleaned and cut into tiny pieces
2 eggs, beaten
2 tablespoons fish sauce
1$^1/_4$ cups (300 ml) coconut milk
$^1/_2$ cup (20 g) finely chopped Thai basil leaves (*horapa*)
2 tablespoons very thinly sliced kaffir lime leaves
Coriander leaves (cilantro) to garnish
1 thinly sliced red chili
Banana leaf cups 2 in (5 cm) square (see instructions below) or heatproof cake pan

Spice Paste
10–15 dried chilies, slit open lengthwise, deseeded and soaked in water
3 cloves garlic
4 slices galangal
1 teaspoon grated kaffir lime rind
2 teaspoons chopped cilantro root
5 black peppercorns
$^1/_2$ teaspoon salt
1 teaspoon dried shrimp paste, roasted (page 21)
1 teaspoon chopped *krachai* (optional)

1 Mix coconut cream with the rice flour and bring to the boil, stirring until thickened. Remove from the heat and set aside to cool for topping.
2 Grind the Spice Paste ingredients in a blender or a mortar and pestle. Mix the Spice Paste with the fish, shrimp, squid, egg and fish sauce. Then add the coconut milk, a little at a time. Add half the basil and kaffir lime leaves and mix in.
3 Place one of the remaining basil leaves in the bottom of each cup or at the bottom of a heatproof baking dish, fill with the seafood mixture, cover and steam for 15 minutes.
4 Remove the cups from the steamer, and top each one with a little of the boiled coconut cream, coriander leaves, kaffir lime leaf and sliced chili.
5 Return to the steamer, cook for 1 more minute, then remove from the steamer.

Note: If you cannot obtain rice flour, you can make rice flour from rice by following the recipe on page 32, or substitute with sifted wheat flour.

Serves 6   Preparation time: 40 mins   Cooking time: 25 mins

To make the banana leaf cups, cut out two circles 4 in (10 cm) in diameter from banana leaf.

Placing one circle on top of the other, make a fold along the outer edges of the circles and secure it with a toothpick.

Make 3 more folds equal distance apart and secure with toothpicks.

Deep-fried Shrimp Cakes   Taud Man Goong

Street vendors in coastal towns, especially around Songkhla, Surat Thani and Phuket, offer a highly seasoned version of this snack made with fish (Taud Man Pla). The more delicate recipe given here is prepared with shrimp and served with a tangy accompaniment of Sweet and Spicy Pickled Vegetables. For interesting variations, try this recipe with crab, crayfish or lobster.

1¹/₄ lbs (600 g) fresh shrimp or prawns, shelled and deveined
¹/₃ cup (2 oz/50 g) ground pork or chopped ham or bacon or 1 tablespoon vegetable oil
1 teaspoon salt
¹/₂ teaspoon sugar
1 cup bread crumbs
2 kaffir lime leaves, very thinly sliced
4 cups (1 liter) oil for deep-frying

Sweet and Spicy Pickled Vegetables
1 cup (250 ml) distilled white vinegar
¹/₂ cup (100 g) sugar
3–5 bird's-eye chilies
3–5 shallots, sliced
2 tablespoons finely sliced cauliflower
2 tablespoons finely sliced baby corn or cabbage
2 tablespoons sliced baby cucumber
1 tablespoon grated ginger

1 To prepare the Sweet and Spicy Pickled Vegetables, bring the vinegar and sugar to a boil, then set aside to cool. Add the remaining ingredients, mix and set aside.
2 Finely chop the shrimp and pork or oil together or process in a blender until they form a rough paste. Add salt, sugar, kaffir lime leaves, and half the bread crumbs, then shape into flat, round patties. Coat the outside of the patties with the remaining bread crumbs.
3 Place the oil in a pan or wok and heat. Deep-fry the patties in the oil until golden brown and fragrant.
4 Serve hot with the Sweet and Spicy Pickled Vegetables and Green Chili Sauce (page 22).

Note: The Sweet and Spicy Pickled Vegetables and shrimp cake patties can be prepared in advance and fried just before serving.

Serves 4   Preparation time: 30 mins   Cooking time: 20 mins

Add the salt, sugar and bread crumbs to the chopped shrimp and pork fat.

Shape the ingredients into small, round patties.

Heat the oil in a wok then deep-fry the patties.

Crispy Prawns with Sweet and Sour Sauce Sakuna Chomsuan

A simple but always popular appetizer that can be prepared with prawns or shrimp. The prawns may be prepared in advance and deep-fried just before serving.

1 lb (500 g) fresh prawns or shrimp
1 egg, lightly beaten
1 cup (100 g) fine bread crumbs
Cooking oil for deep frying

Sweet and Sour Sauce
$1/_2$ in (1 cm) fresh ginger, peeled
2–3 whole shallots, peeled
4 tablespoons white vinegar
3 tablespoons sugar
$1/_2$ teaspoon salt
2 tablespoons (40 g) tomato ketchup
1–2 tablespoons (40 g) hot sauce
 (Sriracha or Tabasco)

1 Peel the prawns, discarding the heads but leaving the tail sections intact. Devein and flatten into a butterfly shape by pressing gently with the hand.
2 To prepare the Sweet and Sour Sauce, grill the ginger and shallots under the broiler, turning until brown on all sides, about 8 minutes. Place the ginger, shallots, vinegar, sugar, salt and ketchup in a pan and bring to a boil. Reduce to medium heat and simmer until all the sugar has dissolved. Remove the ginger and shallots from the pan. Bring to a boil again, then add the hot sauce. Simmer until just thickened, then remove from the heat. Set aside to cool.
3 Heat one finger of oil in a medium saucepan. Dip the shrimp in the egg and bread crumbs. Deep-fry until golden brown and serve with the Sweet and Sour Sauce.

Serves 4   Preparation time: 15 mins   Cooking time: 40 mins

Spicy Prawn Soup with Lemongrass   Tom Yam Goong

One of the best known Thai dishes abroad, this flavorful but spicy soup is hot, sour and fragrant, an ideal accompaniment to other Thai dishes and rice. The kaffir lime leaves, galangal and lemon grass are what give this soup its tangy flavor, but are not meant to be eaten, so tell your guests to avoid them while eating the broth, prawns and mushrooms.

4 cups (1 liter) Thai Chicken Stock (page 22)
3 kaffir lime leaves
2 in (5 cm) fresh galangal root, sliced
3–4 coriander roots, washed (optional)
3 stems lemongrass, thick bottom part only, dry outer sheath discarded, smashed with back of a cleaver
6–8 medium prawns or shrimp, shells intact
1 cup (5 oz/150 g) fresh or canned straw mushrooms or small button mushrooms, sliced in half
5–10 bird's-eye chilies, smashed
3 tablespoons lime juice, or to taste
$1/2$ tablespoon fish sauce, or to taste
3 sprigs fresh coriander leaves (cilantro)

1 Bring the stock to a boil and add kaffir lime leaves, galangal, coriander roots and lemongrass. Simmer for 15 minutes.
2 Add the prawns or shrimp, mushrooms and chilies, and simmer for 3 minutes. Add the lime juice and fish sauce (which is very salty) to taste. The soup should be spicy-sour and a little salty. Serve garnished with fresh coriander leaves (cilantro).

Note: Do not overcook the prawns or they will become tough. Use homemade chicken stock in this dish for the best flavor. Any variety of seafood may be substituted for or added to the prawns—including sliced fish, crab or squid.

Serves 4   Preparation time: 10 mins   Cooking time: 30 mins

Clear Soup with Glass Noodles   Gaeng Jued Woon Sen

Gaeng jued (literally "plain soup") is clear and mild, serving as a contrast to accompanying dishes that are either oily or spicy.

5 oz (150 g) ground pork or chicken
1/2 teaspoon soy sauce
1/4 teaspoon ground white pepper
4 cups (1 liter) Thai Chicken Stock
   (page 22)
3 white peppercorns, crushed
5 cloves garlic, crushed
2 oz (50 g) dried glass noodles (bean
   thread or cellophane noodles),
   soaked in warm water to soften
1 teaspoon fish sauce
6 dried Chinese mushrooms, soaked
   in hot water to soften, stems discarded, tops sliced
1/4 teaspoon sugar
1 spring onion, cut into 1/2 in (1 cm)
   pieces
2 tablespoons chopped coriander
   leaves (cilantro)

1 Mix the meat, soy sauce and ground white pepper together well, and form into small, roughly shaped meatballs.
2 Heat the chicken stock in a pot, add the crushed peppercorns and garlic, and bring to a boil. Place the meat balls in the boiling stock and then add the noodles, fish sauce, mushrooms and sugar. Simmer until the meatballs are cooked. Add the spring onions and coriander leaves and remove from the heat immediately. Serve accompanied by rice.

Note: Glass noodles are soaked in warm water for about 5 minutes to soften and swell.

Serves 4   Preparation time: 10 mins   Cooking time: 8 mins

Stuffed Baby Cucumber Soup   Gaeng Jued Taeng Kwa Yad Sai

3 baby or Japanese cucumbers,
   peeled and sliced into sections
8 oz (225 g) ground pork or chicken
1 egg, lightly beaten
1 tablespoon fish sauce
1/2 teaspoon salt
1/4 teaspoon ground white pepper
1 sprig fresh coriander leaves
   (cilantro), roughly chopped
4 cups (1 liter) Thai Chicken Stock
   (page 22)
Handful (2 oz/50 g) dried glass noodles (bean thread or cellophane
   noodles), soaked in warm water for
   5 minutes to soften (optional)
1 spring onion, cut into 1/2-in (1-cm)
   pieces

1 Scoop out the center of the cucumber sections, taking care not to cut through the outer flesh. Set the cucumbers aside.
2 Mix the ground meat with the egg, fish sauce, salt, pepper and coriander leaves (cilantro). Reserve some leaves as garnish.
3 Stuff the cucumbers with the meat mixture, then steam them in a bamboo or metal steamer over high heat for about 15 minutes.
4 Heat the chicken stock in a pot over medium heat. Add the steamed cucumber sections and cook until heated through. Then add the glass noo-dles, if desired. Garnish with the spring onion and the remainer of the coriander leaves, and serve hot.

Serves 4   Preparation time: 20 mins   Cooking time: 20 mins

Seafood Soup with Basil   Poh Taek

Thailand's abundance of seafood makes mixed seafood dishes a delight. The wonderful flavor of this soup is enhanced by the use of lime juice, herbs and galangal.

4–5 cups Thai Chicken Stock (page 22)
1 fresh crab, cleaned, back shell discarded, body cut into 6 pieces (optional)
2 stems lemongrass, thick bottom half only, bruised
3 in (8 cm) galangal root, peeled and sliced
3 kaffir lime leaves
5 oz (150 g) white fish fillet, cleaned and cut into bite-sized pieces
6 medium shrimp or prawns
6 mussels in their shells, cleaned well
6 oz (170 g) squid, cleaned and cut into $^3/_4$-in (2-cm) slices
2 tablespoons fish sauce, or to taste
$^1/_4$ teaspoon palm sugar, shaved
1 tablespoon lime juice, or to taste
Handful Thai basil leaves (*horapa*)
4–8 green bird's-eye chilies, crushed

1 Bring chicken stock to a boil. Add crab if using, and return to a boil.
2 Add lemon grass, galangal and kaffir lime leaves, then add fish, shrimps, mussels, and squid. Cook for another 5 minutes, then remove from the heat.
3 Add fish sauce, sugar and lemon juice to taste. Garnish with basil and chillies, and serve in bowls accompanied by rice, fish sauce and lemon juice.

Serves 6   Preparation time: 20 mins   Cooking time: 17 mins

Creamy Chicken Soup with Coconut Milk   Tom Kha Gai

A delightful soup, rich with coconut milk and fragrant with the elusive flavor of galangal. Reduce the amount of chilies if you don't want the soup to be too spicy.

4 cups Thai Chicken Stock (page 22)
2 stems lemongrass, thick bottom
half only, dry outer sheath removed,
smashed with the back of a cleaver
2 in (5 cm) galangal root, peeled and
sliced thinly
3 kaffir lime leaves, torn into small
pieces
12 oz (350 g) boneless chicken, cut
into small pieces
12 fresh or canned straw mushrooms
or small button mushrooms, sliced
in half
1 teaspoon salt
4 tablespoons lime juice
3 tablespoons fish sauce
$1/2$ teaspoon sugar
3 cups thin coconut milk
2–3 red bird's-eye chilies, bruised

1 Place the stock in a pot and add the lemongrass, galangal and kaffir lime leaves. Bring to a boil over medium heat. Add the chicken, mushrooms, salt, lime juice, fish sauce and sugar. Reduce heat to low and cook slowly, uncovered, for 10 minutes or until the chicken changes color, then add coconut milk and chilies. Bring almost to a boil, stirring constantly for 2–3 minutes, then remove from heat and serve.

Note: Cook gently over very low heat at the final stages to prevent the coconut milk from separating.

Serves 4–6   Preparation time: 20 mins   Cooking time: 20 mins

Sour Seafood Soup with Vegetables Gaeng Som

Sour but fragrant tamarind juice adds a special touch to this relatively mild soup, which is chock-full of vegetables, prawns or shrimp, and chopped fish. As with other types of *gaeng*, this has very little liquid.

3 cups (750 ml) water
8 oz (250 g) fresh white fish fillets
4 oz (100 g) fresh prawns or shrimp
12 fresh or canned straw mushrooms or small button mushrooms, sliced in half
$1/2$ cup (125 g) sliced daikon radish
$1/2$ cup (125 g) sliced green papaya
$1/2$ cup (60 g) sliced green beans
$1/2$ cup (60 g) cauliflower, broken into florets
$1/2$ cup (125 g) sliced Chinese cabbage
4 tablespoons tamarind juice (page 21)
2 tablespoons lime juice (optional)
1 tablespoon chopped palm sugar or dark brown sugar
1 teaspoon salt

Spice Paste
3 dried chilies, deseeded and soaked until soft
2 teaspoons chopped garlic
2 teaspoons chopped shallots
1 teaspoon chopped *krachai* (optional)

1 Bring the water to a boil in a large pot.
2 Place the fish fillets and prawns or shrimp in the boiling water and simmer for about 8 minutes until cooked. Use a slotted spoon and remove the seafood. Let it cool. Chop up the fish. Reserve the stock and set the seafood aside.
3 Grind the Spice Paste ingredients in a blender or mortar and pestle, then place the Spice Paste in a pan with the reserved stock, fish and vegetables. Bring to a boil and simmer until just cooked, about 10 minutes. Add the tamarind juice, lime juice, sugar and salt.
4 Serve hot topped with prawns or shrimp.

Note: Any combination of vegetables can be used; suggested alternatives include chayote, any other type of summer squash or zucchini, eggplant, green cabbage, and button mushrooms.

Serves 4–6   Preparation time: 30 mins   Cooking time: 25 mins

Green Papaya Salad Som Tam Thai

Originally an Isan dish from the northeast, this healthy mixture of raw vegetables is now prepared by roadside vendors all over the country. Som Tam captures the essential flavors of Thailand: chili hot, redolent with garlic and fish sauce, and sour with lime juice. The basic ingredient, unripe papaya, contrasts in texture with crunchy raw beans and peanuts. If unripe papaya is not available, very thinly sliced cabbage may be substituted.

2–5 bird's-eye chilies
2 tablespoons unsalted roasted peanuts or cashew nuts
1 tablespoon dried shrimp or prawns, soaked in warm water for
  5 minutes and drained
5 cloves garlic
10 oz (300 g) unripe green papaya, peeled and shredded using
  a sharp knife or vegetable grater
$^1/_2$ cup (50 g) long beans or green beans, cut in $^1/_2$-in (1-cm) pieces
6 ripe cherry tomatoes, quartered, or 1 large tomato, in wedges
3 tablespoons lime juice
1 tablespoon chopped palm sugar or dark brown sugar

1 tablespoon fish sauce
2 cups raw vegetables (cabbage, water spinach, broccoli, asparagus)
3 sprigs Thai basil (*horapa*)

1 Take the chilies, peanuts, dried shrimp and garlic and pound roughly in a mortar and pestle or process very briefly in a blender. The mixture should be coarse, not smooth.
2 Combine mixture in a bowl with the shredded papaya, beans and tomato. Mix well and add the lime juice, palm sugar and fish sauce.
3 Serve accompanied by other raw vegetables (cabbage, water spinach, broccoli or asparagus) and sprigs of Thai basil. For a complete meal, add glutinous rice and Barbecued Chicken (page 84).

Note: Prepare the salad immediately before serving, otherwise the papaya will lose its firm texture.

Serves 4   Preparation time: 30 mins

Spicy Pomelo or Grapefruit Salad   Yam Som-O

Large round pomelos, the Asian equivalent of grapefruit, are generally bitter-sweet, and are eaten as a fruit as well as mixed with sour, spicy ingredients and shrimp or chicken to make a salad. A favorite Thai snack is to just dip segments of pomelo into whatever sauce happens to be available. This salad goes well with rice and other cooked dishes.

1 pomelo or 2 large grapefruits
2 tablespoons lime juice
1 tablespoon fish sauce
1 tablespoon sugar
5 oz (150 g) boiled or grilled prawns
  or shrimp, shells removed
2 cups (200 g) cooked chicken
  breast, shredded
2 tablespoons grated fresh or dried
  unsweetened coconut
$1/_2$–1 tablespoon dried shrimp or
  prawns, soaked in warm water for
  5 minutes and drained, lightly
  pounded or processed
1 dried chili, seeded and chopped
$1/_4$ cup (60 ml) coconut cream
  (optional)

1 Peel the pomelo and shred the flesh, removing the seeds. (If using grapefruit, peel and section, removing all the skins.)
2 Place the lime juice, fish sauce and sugar in a bowl and stir well to dissolve the sugar. Then add the prawns or shrimp, chicken and grated coconut. Mix well.
3 Add the pomelo or grapefruit and grated coconut. Toss lightly.
4 Serve sprinkled with chopped dried shrimp and chili, and drizzled with a little coconut cream, if using.

Note: If you are using grapefruit, it may be necessary to add extra sugar.

Serves 4   Preparation time: 17 mins   Cooking time: 12 mins

Glass Noodle Salad   Yam Woon Sen

4 oz (100 g) dried glass noodles (cellophane or bean thread noodles),
soaked in warm water for 15 minutes, drained and cut into sections
1 chicken breast (12 oz/375 g),
poached and shredded
1 tablespoon dried shrimps, soaked
in warm water for 5 minutes, drained
and lightly pounded or processed
$^1/_2$ stalk Chinese celery, chopped
$^1/_2$ carrot, coarsely grated
$^1/_4$ cup thinly sliced red onion or
shallots
1 cup (110 g) beansprouts, raw or
lightly blanched
1 spring onion, chopped
1 sprig coriander leaves (cilantro),
roughly chopped
$^1/_2$ cup (10 g) fresh mint leaves
3 tablespoons fresh lime juice
3 tablespoons fish sauce
1–2 chillies, seeded and coarsely
chopped or pounded
2 tablespoons chopped roasted
peanuts

1 Blanch the glass noodles, remove from the saucepan, and rinse under
cold water until cool. Drain thoroughly.
2 Place the noodles in a mixing bowl. Add the remaining ingredients except
the peanuts. Stir to combine well. Arrange on a serving platter and garnish
with the peanuts.

Serves 4   Preparation time: 20 mins   Cooking time: 15 mins

Grilled Beef Salad Yum Nua

This salad is an ideal way to use up any leftover roast or grilled beef. Lamb may also be substituted for a delightful variation on this classic dish. Lettuce is often added to this dish although in Thailand it is often served mainly with cucumber, Chinese celery and herbs (mint and coriander leaves).

1 lb (450 g) beef sirloin or leftover roast or steak
1 tablespoon uncooked long grain or jasmine rice
$1/2$ cup sliced cucumber
$1/2$ cup sliced Chinese celery
1 large tomato or 6 cherry tomatoes, sliced
5–7 shallots, thinly sliced
$1/2$ cup mint and coriander leaves (cilantro) to garnish
Small head of lettuce (optional), washed and torn

Dressing
2 tablespoons lime juice
1 tablespoon fish sauce
3 teaspoons sugar
$1/2$ teaspoon crushed dried chilies or ground red pepper

1 If using uncooked beef fillet, sear, chargrill or roast the beef to taste, then slice thinly and set aside.
2 Dry roast the rice grains in a wok or pan over medium heat until lightly browned. Remove from the pan and grind the roasted rice lightly in a mortar and pestle or blender. Set aside.
3 Mix all the Dressing ingredients in a large mixing bowl. Add the sliced beef, cucumber, Chinese celery, tomato wedges and shallots to the bowl and toss to coat. Add the lettuce (if using) and toss again.
4 Transfer to a serving dish and serve garnished with the roasted rice, mint and coriander leaves (cilantro).

Serves 4   Preparation time: 20 mins   Cooking time: 10 mins

Chicken Salad with Vegetables Lab Gai

This dish makes a wonderfully healthy dish because it is made without oil and eaten with raw vegetables and herbs (and rice). It may be served with a chili sauce like Nam Jim (page 22).

10 oz (300 g) ground chicken
3 cloves garlic, finely chopped
$^1/_4$ cup (60 ml) fresh lime or lemon juice
$1^1/_2$ tablespoons fish sauce
2 tablespoons uncooked long grain or jasmine rice
2–3 bird's-eye chillies, minced
1 medium onion, thinly sliced
2 spring onions, chopped
2 sprigs coriander leaves (cilantro), finely chopped
1 cup (20 g) fresh mint leaves
An assortment of lettuce leaves, cabbage, fresh Thai basil (*horapa*), cucumber and
  long beans or green beans

1 Dry roast the rice grains in a wok or pan over medium heat until lightly browned. Remove from the pan and grind the roasted rice lightly in a mortar and pestle or blender. Set aside.
2 Cook the meat and garlic without oil in a non-stick wok or frying pan over medium heat until the meat turns white. Remove from the heat to cool.
3 Add the lime juice, fish sauce and salt, stirring to mix well. Stir in the rice powder, minced chillies, onion, scallion, cilantro and mint leaves.
4 Arrange the chicken mixture on a serving platter and surround the chicken with raw vegetables and herbs, as desired.

Serves 4–6   Preparation time: 10 mins   Cooking time: 15 mins

Stir-fried Mixed Vegetables   Pad Pak Ruam Mit

This method of cooking vegetables can be used for individual vegetables, such as Chinese broccoli, or almost any combination of vegetables depending on availability and preference.

8 oz (225 g) Chinese broccoli
   (*kailan*) or broccoli stems
3–4 cabbage leaves, sliced
$^1/_2$ cup (100 g) sliced carrots
$^1/_2$ cup (100 g) cauliflower florets
$^1/_2$ cup (50 g) snow peas
$^1/_2$ cup (50 g) baby sweet corn
2 tablespoons oil
3 tablespoons minced garlic
5 fresh shiitake or Chinese mushrooms, stems removed and sliced
$^1/_2$ cup (125 ml) Thai Chicken Stock
   (page 22) or water
3 tablespoons oyster sauce
$^1/_2$ tablespoon soy sauce
$^1/_2$ teaspoon black soy sauce
1 tablespoon fish sauce
Dash of rice wine, sherry or sake
$^1/_2$ teaspoon ground white pepper
$^1/_2$ teaspoon sugar

1 Heat a wok until lightly smoking and add the oil. When hot, add the garlic and stir well for 1 minute, or until fragrant. Add mushrooms and stir-fry for 1 minute.
2 Add the vegetables and chicken stock or water to the wok and stir-fry for about 8–10 minutes until just cooked; the vegetables should still be slightly crisp. Add the oyster, soy and fish sauces and wine, then sprinkle with pepper and sugar. Mix well and cook for 1 minute.
3 Serve accompanied by rice.

Note: Use maximum heat to stir fry the vegetables to ensure the right texture and flavor. If using dried Chinese mushrooms, soak in warm water for 15 minutes before slicing.

Serves 6–8   Preparation time: 20 mins   Cooking time: 7 mins

Chinese Broccoli with Crispy Pork or Bacon   Kana Moo Grob

Vegetables are frequently cooked with a little meat, poultry or seafood to add flavor and a contrasting texture. Chinese broccoli or kale, known in Thailand by its Chinese name, *kailan*, is enjoyed for its crunchy stems. If this vegetable is not available, try using broccoli stems instead.

10 oz (300 g) Chinese broccoli
   (*kailan*) or broccoli stems
3 tablespoons oil
1 tablespoon minced garlic
4 tablespoons oyster sauce
$1/4$ teaspoon salt
$1/4$ teaspoon ground white pepper
1 teaspoon sugar
$1/2$ cup (125 ml) Thai Chicken Stock
   (page 22) or water
5 oz (150 g) crispy roasted pork or
   bacon, sliced into bite-sized pieces

1 Discard the leaves and tough bottom part of the broccoli stems. Peel the skin off the tender stems and discard. Cut stems in 2 to 3-in (5 to 8-cm) lengths.
2 Heat the oil in a wok. When it is very hot, fry the garlic until fragrant, about 1 minute, then add the broccoli and stir-fry for 5–6 minutes. Add all the seasonings and stock. Add the crispy pork and stir-fry to heat through. Do not overcook.
3 Serve immediately.

Note: Roasted pork with a layer of meat, a thin layer of fat and crisp, golden-brown skin, contrasts beautifully in taste and texture with the broccoli. Although unconventional, thick slices of crisp fried bacon make an excellent substitute. One lb of bacon, cooked until crisp, will yield approximately 5 oz (150 g) of cooked meat.

Serves 4   Preparation time: 10 mins   Cooking time: 15 mins

Stir-fried Water Spinach   Pak Bung Fai Dtaeng

2 tablespoons oil
3 garlic cloves, peeled and crushed
1 long red chili, thinly sliced
1 tablespoon salted fermented bean
  sauce (*tao jiew*)
12 oz (350 g) water spinach, washed
  well to remove grit and torn into
  sections
2 teaspoons sugar
1 tablespoon soy sauce
2 teaspoons fish sauce

1 Heat a wok until very hot then add the oil. When oil is hot, add garlic and stir-fry until fragrant, about 1 minute. Add the chili and fermented bean sauce and stir-fry until bean sauce is evenly mixed.
2 Add the water spinach, sugar, soy sauce and fish sauce. Stir-fry until the spinach is just wilted, 2–3 minutes. Transfer to a plate and serve hot.

Note: It is important to measure out all the sauces before cooking, as this dish cooks very fast.

Serves 4   Preparation time: 10 mins   Cooking time: 5 mins

Stir-fried Asparagus with Shrimp   Pat Nor Mai Farang

2 tablespoons oil
3 cloves garlic, peeled and minced
10 oz (300 g) young asparagus, cut
   into bite-sized lengths
5 oz (150 g) shrimp, peeled and
   deveined, tails intact
1 teaspoon soy sauce
2 teaspoons oyster sauce
1 teaspoon fish sauce
$^1/_4$ teaspoon sugar
$^1/_2$ cup Thai Chicken Stock (page 22)
1 teaspoon cornstarch mixed in
   2 tablespoons water
$^1/_4$ teaspoon ground white pepper

1 Heat a wok until very hot then add the oil. When oil is hot, add garlic and stir-fry until fragrant, about 1 minute. Add asparagus and shrimp and stir-fry until asparagus is just tender and shrimp turn pink, 3–4 minutes.
2 Add soy sauce, oyster sauce, fish sauce and sugar. Stir-fry then add Thai Chicken Stock and cornstarch mixture and simmer for 1 minute.
3 Transfer to a plate, sprinkle with pepper and serve hot.

Note: It is important to measure out all the sauces before cooking, as this dish cooks very fast.

Serves 6   Preparation time: 10 mins   Cooking time: 5 mins

Southern-style Rice Salad   Khao Yam Pak Tai

This is a popular way of using leftover rice and makes an ideal light luncheon dish. The seasonings added to the rice can be varied according to taste and availability; not all ingredients used in the following recipe are shown in the photograph opposite.

2 cups (320 g) cooked rice
1 cup (90 g) grated coconut, browned in an oven or dry-roasted in a pan
 for 5–8 minutes
1 small pomelo or grapefruit, peeled and sectioned
1 small green mango, grated (optional)
$^1/_2$ cup (80 g) dried shrimp, soaked and lightly pounded or processed
$^1/_2$ cup (50 g) raw bean sprouts
$^1/_2$ cup (80 g) finely sliced lemongrass (inner part of thick end of stem only)
$^1/_4$ cup (25 g) sliced green beans
1 egg, beaten, cooked into an omelet and thinly sliced
2 dried red chilies, seeded and finely sliced or pounded
1 tablespoon very finely sliced kaffir lime leaf
$^1/_2$ cup chopped coriander leaves (cilantro) or Thai basil leaves (horapa)
4 oz (100 g) cooked prawns as garnish (optional)
1 spring onion, minced
Lime wedges

Sauce
$^1/_2$ cup (125 ml) water
2 tablespoons chopped salted fish or anchovies in brine
1 tablespoon chopped palm sugar or dark brown sugar
2 kaffir lime leaves, very thinly sliced
1 tablespoon lemongrass (inner part of thick end of stem
 only), very finely sliced

1 Put all the Sauce ingredients in a pan, bring to a boil and simmer for
5 minutes. Remove from heat, strain and set aside.
2 Place the rice in small bowls, each holding about half a cup. Press down then invert onto a large serving platter. Arrange the rest of the raw ingredients around the edge of rice in separate piles.
3 To eat, spoon some rice onto individual plates and take a little of each ingredient to mix with the rice according to taste. Spoon the sauce over the top.

Note: Canned anchovies packed in Europe make an acceptable substitute for the preserved Thai variety. If the very fine dried shrimp used in Thailand are not available, substitute with packaged fish floss.

Serves 4   Preparation time: 20 mins   Cooking time: 15 mins

Shrimp Fried Rice *Khao Pad Goong*

3 tablespoons oil
4 cloves garlic, minced
1 slice bacon, thinly sliced
8 oz (250 g) fresh prawns or shrimp, peeled and deveined
3 eggs, beaten
4 cups cooked white rice, cooled
2 tablespoons fish sauce
1 tablespoon soy sauce
$1/_2$ tablespoon sugar
$1/_4$ teaspoon white pepper
$1/_2$ cup sliced onion
1 spring onion, chopped
2 tablespoons chopped coriander leaves (cilantro)

Accompaniments
Sliced cucumbers
Sliced tomatoes
Chopped spring onions
Sliced chillies
Fish sauce

1 Heat a large wok or skillet until smoking and add the oil. Add the garlic and stir-fry for 1 minute or until fragrant. Add the bacon and shrimps and stir-fry for 1 minute or until shrimps turn pink.
2 Add the eggs and scramble until cooked. Add the rice, fish and soy sauces, sugar and white pepper. Continue to stir-fry until the rice is hot, reducing the temperature if necessary. Add onion and spring onions.
3 Garnish with coriander leaves and serve with Accompaniments.

Serves 4   Preparation time: 10 mins   Cooking time: 8 mins

Fried Rice Sticks with Shrimp Pad Thai Goong Sod

Dried rice-flour noodles are used for this dish, one of the dozens of noodle creations found in Thailand. The pickled Chinese radish is available in cans, usually packed in China.

5 tablespoons oil
1 cake pressed bean curd, diced
5 cloves garlic, minced
5 shallots, minced
1 tablespoon dried shrimps or prawns, soaked for 5 minutes in warm water and drained, lightly pounded or processed
1 tablespoon chopped pickled Chinese radish
10 oz (300 g) dried rice-stick noodles, soaked in warm water to soften, drained well
1 teaspoon dried chili flakes or ground red pepper
3 eggs
2 cups bean sprouts, cleaned
$1/_4$ cup garlic chives or spring onions, sliced into 1-in (2-cm) lengths
2 tablespoons crushed peanuts
5 oz (150g) fresh prawns or shrimps, peeled and deveined, and grilled

Sauce
3 tablespoons shaved palm sugar
3 tablespoons fish sauce
3 tablespoons tamarind pulp soaked in $1/_2$ cup water, then strained to remove seeds and fibers

1 Place all the Sauce ingredients in a small saucepan and bring to a boil. Reduce heat and simmer for 3–5 minutes. Remove from heat and set aside.
2 Heat 3 tablespoons oil in a large pan and stir-fry bean curd till lightly brown, about 5 minutes. Drain and set aside.
3 Stir-fry garlic and shallots over high heat for 2 minutes. Add dried shrimps and pickled radish and fry for another 3 minutes. Add noodles and bean curd and stir-fry to mix, then add Sauce and dried chili flakes. Continue to stir-fry over medium heat.
4 Push noodles to one side. Add 2 tablespoons oil, break the eggs into the pan and scramble till cooked, then mix eggs and noodles together.
5 Add half the bean sprouts and garlic chives or spring onions. Mix together thoroughly and remove from heat.
6 Serve garnished with the remaining bean sprouts and chives, crushed peanuts and grilled shrimp, if using.

Note: Fried noodles require a lot of oil; however, it is possible to use a minimum amount by adding small amounts from time to time to keep the noodles from drying out instead of adding all the oil at once.

Serves 4–6   Preparation time: 15 mins   Cooking time: 15 mins

Stir-fry garlic, shallots, dried shrimps and pickled radish, then add the rice-stick noodles to the wok.

Add bean curd, followed by Sauce. Stir-fry to mix thoroughly.

Push noodles to one side. Add more oil, break eggs into the pan and scramble till cooked.

Northern-style Chicken Noodle Soup Khao Soi

This Burmese-influenced dish, with a curry-like gravy bathing the chicken and noodles, is very popular at lunch time in Chiang Mai and other northern towns.

4 cups (1 liter) thin coconut milk
10 oz (300 g) boneless chicken breast, skin removed and meat cut in thin slices
1 tablespoon soy sauce
1 tablespoon black soy sauce
$^1/_2$ teaspoon salt
12 oz (400 g) dried egg noodles
3 cups oil for deep-frying
6 cups (1$^1/_2$ liter) water

Chili Paste
4 dried chilies, deseeded and sliced
2 tablespoons sliced shallots
3 teaspoons sliced ginger
2 teaspoons coriander seeds
Pea-sized knob of fresh turmeric, or 1 teaspoon turmeric powder

Accompaniments
2 tablespoons sliced shallots
$^1/_4$ cup (40 g) salted cabbage
1 tablespoon dried chili flakes

1 Make the Chili Paste first by dry-roasting all ingredients in a skillet over low heat for about 8 to 10 minutes until fragrant, then grind in a blender or mortar until fine.
2 Heat 1 cup (250 ml) of the coconut milk in a saucepan or wok over medium heat, add the chili paste and cook for 2 minutes. Add the chicken and soy sauces and cook for 3 minutes, stirring frequently, or until the chicken changes color. Then add the rest of the coconut milk and bring to a boil. Reduce heat to low and simmer for 3 minutes, then add the salt and remove from the heat. Set aside.
3 Heat oil in a saucepan until very hot and deep-fry 4 oz (125 g) of the dried noodles until crisp. Quickly remove and drain well.
4 Boil the rest of the noodles in water until cooked but still slightly firm, about 4–5 minutes, then drain.
5 Place the boiled noodles in serving bowls and pour the chicken and coconut mixture on top. Garnish with the fried noodles and serve with the Accompaniments, allowing each person to add a little according to taste.

Note: Salted cabbage is usually available at Chinese provision stores. Alternatively, salted mustard greens make a good substitute.

Serves 4   Preparation time: 10 mins   Cooking time: 40 mins

Rice Noodles with Coconut Fish Curry   Kanom Jeen Nam Yaa

An excellent and tasty light meal, using the fresh round rice-flour noodles known as *kanom jeen*. Because of their length, *kanom jeen* are commonly served at family ceremonies, including marriages and birthdays; never broken until served, they signify long life. If fresh rice-flour noodles are not available, use dried rice vermicelli or rice sticks.

1 lb (500 g) fresh round rice noodles (*kanom jeen*) or 10 oz (300 g) dried rice vermicelli or rice sticks, blanched in boiling water for 2–3 minutes
2 hard-boiled eggs, peeled and quartered
1/2 cup (75 g) sliced cabbage
1/2 cup (90 g) sliced cucumber
1/2 cup (50 g) blanched bean sprouts
1 small bunch lemon basil (*manglak*)
1 tablespoon dried chili flakes

Coconut Fish Curry
1 small, fresh fish, about 8 oz (250 g)
1/3 cup (75 g) sliced shallots
2 cloves garlic
2 thick slices galangal root
2 tablespoons sliced lemongrass (inner part of thick half of stem only)
1 cup (150 g) minced *krachai* (optional)
3 dried chilies, seeds removed
1 teaspoon salt
1 teaspoon dried shrimp paste, roasted
1 cup (250 ml) water
4 cups (1 liter) thin coconut milk
2–3 tablespoons fish sauce
1/2 cup (250 ml) coconut cream

1 To make the Coconut Fish Curry, first wash and clean the fish, removing head. Place in a small pot, cover with a small amount of water, and simmer covered until soft. Drain and reserve the broth. Allow the fish to cool and remove the flesh, discarding the skin and bones. Set aside.
2 Place shallots, garlic, galangal, lemongrass, *krachai* (if using), chilies, salt, shrimp paste and water in a pot and simmer over low heat until soft, about 10 minutes. Remove from heat, cool and transfer to a blender or mortar and pestle. Add the fish and grind to a paste.
3 Put the ground mixture into a pot and add the coconut milk. Bring to a boil, then add the fish broth and fish sauce. Reduce heat to low and simmer, stirring regularly to prevent sticking, until the sauce has thickened and the surface glistens. Add the coconut cream and remove from heat.
4 Arrange a portion of the rice noodles and a little of each of the other ingredients in individual bowls. Spoon the Coconut Fish Curry over the noodles just before serving.

Serves 4   Preparation time: 15 mins   Cooking time: 60 mins

Rice Stick Noodles with Seafood and Basil   Kwaytiaow Pad Leemao Thalay

Kwaytiaow or flat rice stick noodles, Chinese in origin, are now enthusiastically enjoyed in most parts of Thailand. They are served either in soups or stir-fried with meat or seafood, vegetables and spices. This version is understandably popular in coastal areas where a wide variety of seafood is available.

1 lb (500 g) mixed raw or cooked
  seafood such as squid, prawns,
  fish, clams and mussels, cleaned
  and shelled
3 tablespoons minced garlic
2 tablespoons oil
1 lb (500 g) fresh rice-flour noodles
  (*kwaytiaow*) or 10 oz (300 g) dried
  rice sticks soaked in boiling water
  for 5 minutes and thoroughly
  drained
2 tablespoons soy sauce
2 tablespoons fish sauce
$^1/_4$ cup Thai basil leaves (*horapa*)
2 red chilies, thinly sliced
Ground white pepper to taste

1 Cut seafood into bite-sized pieces. Fry the garlic in 2 tablespoons oil in a large wok over high heat until golden brown. Add the seafood and stir-fry for a few minutes. Remove seafood from the wok and set aside.
2 Stir-fry the noodles with soy sauce in the remaining oil for 2 to 3 minutes, then add the cooked seafood back to the wok. Mix well and add fish sauce, basil leaves and chilies. Stir, sprinkle with white pepper to taste and cook for a minute more.

Serves 6–8   Preparation time: 10 mins   Cooking time: 10 mins

Stir-fried Rice Stick Noodles with Minced Beef   Kwaytiaow Nuea Sab

3 tablespoons oil
2 shallots, thinly sliced
5 oz (150 g) ground beef
2 teaspoons soy sauce
2 teaspoons fish sauce
1 teaspoon cornstarch (cornflour),
  blended with 3 tablespoons water
1 teaspoon sugar
1 teaspoon minced garlic
1 lb (500 g) fresh rice-flour noodles
  (*kwaytiaow*) or 10 oz (300 g) dried
  rice sticks soaked in boiling water
  for 5 minutes and thoroughly
  drained
$^1/_2$ tablespoon black soy sauce
$^1/_2$ teaspoon salt
$^1/_2$ teaspoon freshly ground black
  pepper
4–5 quail's eggs, hard-boiled and
  peeled (optional)

Accompaniments
Lettuce leaves
Sliced green chilies in lime juice

1 Heat 1 tablespoon of the oil in a wok. Add the shallots to the pan and fry until transparent. Add the beef and stir-fry for 3 minutes. Add the soy and fish sauces, cornstarch mixture and sugar. Stir-fry for 3 more minutes and set aside.

2 Heat the remaining oil over medium heat, add garlic and fry until fragrant. Add the noodles, dark soy sauce, salt and pepper and stir-fry for 3 minutes. Remove from the heat and place on a serving dish.

3 Top the noodles with the cooked minced beef and the eggs, if desired, and serve accompanied with lettuce and sliced green chilies in lime juice if desired.

Serves 4–6   Preparation time: 15 mins   Cooking time: 10 mins

Green Chicken Curry with Basil and Eggplant Gaeng Kheow Wan Gai

A fragrant, creamy curry which is always popular. Remove the skin from the chicken if you wish to reduce the fat.

1/2 cup (125 ml) coconut cream
3 tablespoons Green Curry Paste
 (page 23)
12 oz (350 g) boneless chicken
 breast, thinly sliced
1 1/2 cups (375 ml) thin coconut milk
2 kaffir lime leaves
1 1/2 tablespoons fish sauce
1 teaspoon sugar
5 oz (150 g) eggplant, cut into bite-
 sized pieces (about 1 1/2 cups)
1/4 cup (10 g) Thai basil leaves
 (horapa)
2–3 red chilies, deseeded and cut in
 strips

1 Place coconut cream in a saucepan and heat over low to medium heat until it begins to have an oily sheen. Add the Green Curry Paste and stir well. Add the chicken and cook until it changes color. Add coconut milk, kaffir lime leaves, fish sauce and sugar. Bring to a boil, then add the eggplant. Simmer over low heat until the chicken is cooked, about 15 minutes, then add the basil and chilies. Remove from heat and serve.

Note: This dish can be prepared in advance by cooking it until the chicken is tender. Add the basil and chilies when reheating the dish just before serving.

Serves 4   Preparation time: 15 mins   Cooking time: 25 mins

Chicken Wrapped in Pandanus Leaves   Gai Hor Bai Toey

Fragrant screwpine or pandanus palm leaves add their subtle fragrance to this deep-fried chicken dish, which is the Thai version of the popular Chinese Chee Pow Gai (Paper-wrapped Chicken).

1 lb (500 g) boneless chicken meat
16 pandanus leaves
Oil for deep-frying

Marinade
2 tablespoons soy sauce
1 tablespoon oyster sauce
1 teaspoon sugar
2 teaspoons sesame oil
2 cloves garlic and 3 coriander roots,
  pounded together to a paste

Sauce
1 teaspoon white sesame seeds
1 cup (250 ml) distilled white vinegar
$^1/_2$ cup (100 g) sugar
2 tablespoons black soy sauce
1 teaspoon fish sauce

1 Cut chicken meat into bite-sized chunks. Mix the Marinade ingredients well into the chicken. Set aside in the refrigerator to marinate for 3 hours.
2 To prepare the Sauce, dry-fry the sesame seeds in a skillet for 2 minutes or until lightly browned. Set aside. Mix the remaining Sauce ingredients together in a bowl, then add the sesame seeds and set aside.
3 Wrap two or three pieces of chicken in each pandanus leaf to form a knot (see photo). Alternatively, wrap each pandanus leaf around the chicken to form a bundle and secure with a toothpick.
4 Heat oil in a wok or small frying pan. Deep-fry until fragrant, about 5 minutes. Serve with Sauce and steamed rice.

Note: If pandanus leaves are not available, add a few drops of pandan essence to the Marinade. Drain the chicken pieces and stir-fry for 5 minutes in 1 tablespoon of oil over medium high heat, and garnish with coriander leaves (cilantro).

Serves 4   Preparation time: 30 mins   Cooking time: 7 mins

Red Chicken Curry with Bamboo Shoots   Gaeng Ped Gai Naw Mai

Fresh bamboo shoots (*naw mai*) are a seasonal delicacy in Thailand, and have a sweetness and texture that cannot quite be matched by the canned variety. However, the latter makes an acceptable substitute, providing a firm contrast to the tender chicken in this curry-style dish.

$1/_2$ cup (125 ml) coconut cream
2 tablespoons Red Curry Paste (page 22)
12 oz (350 g) boneless chicken meat, cut into bite-sized strips
$1^1/_2$ cups (375 ml) thin coconut milk
10 oz (300 g) bamboo shoots, sliced
2 tablespoons fish sauce
$1/_4$ teaspoon salt
$1^1/_2$ teaspoons sugar
5 kaffir lime leaves, halved
1 fresh red chili, thinly sliced
$1/_2$ cup (20 g) Thai basil leaves (*horapa*)

1 If using fresh bamboo shoots, peel and slice and place in a saucepan. Cover with water and boil until just tender, about 5 minutes. (Canned bamboo shoots should be drained, sliced and boiled for 2–3 minutes in a little water to remove any metallic taste.)

2 Bring the coconut cream to a boil in a saucepan over medium heat. Reduce to low heat and simmer, stirring constantly, until the surface takes on an oily sheen. Add the Red Curry Paste and chicken, stir well, and add the coconut milk and bamboo shoots.

3 Continue to simmer over low heat until the chicken is tender, about 10 minutes, then add fish sauce, salt, sugar, kaffir lime leaves and chili. Remove from heat and garnish with basil.

Serves 4   Preparation time: 15 mins   Cooking time: 20 mins

Roast Duck Curry Gaeng Ped

Seasoned red-roasted duck sold by Chinese restaurants and food stores is the basis for this richly-flavored curry.

$^1/_2$ roasted duck (about 1$^1/_2$ lbs/675 g)
$^1/_2$ cup (125 ml) coconut cream
2 tablespoons Red Curry Paste (page 22)
1$^1/_2$ cups (375 ml) thin coconut milk
1 large or 2 small tomatoes, cut in wedges
$^1/_2$ cup seedless grapes or diced pineapple (optional)
1 cup (150 g) pea-sized eggplants, or 1 small eggplant cut into
  bite-sized chunks
3 kaffir lime leaves
2 tablespoons fish sauce
1 teaspoon sugar
$^1/_2$ teaspoon salt
10 Thai basil leaves (*horapa*)
2–4 red or green chilies, cut into strips

1 Remove all bones from the duck and cut the meat into bite-sized pieces.
2 Place the coconut cream in a saucepan and heat over medium heat. Add the Red Curry Paste, stirring well.
3 Add the duck and stir well, then add the coconut milk, tomatoes, eggplant, grapes or pineapple (if using), kaffir lime leaves, fish sauce, sugar and salt. Bring to a boil, then remove from heat.
4 Sprinkle with the basil leaves and red or green chilies. Serve with plain rice.

Note: The pea-sized eggplants add a slightly crunchy texture to the smooth curry, while the grapes or pineapple add a tangy sweetness. If the tomatoes are sour, you may need to add slightly more sugar to compensate.

Serves 4–6   Preparation time: 15 mins   Cooking time: 20 mins

Mussaman Beef Curry   Gaeng Mussaman

Spices such as cloves, cardamom and cinnamon were brought to Thailand by Muslim traders from Java, India and Sumatra, and dishes using these are referred to as Mussaman (Muslim) curries. This version from southern Thailand uses the basic Mussaman Curry Paste and other spices.

$1/_2$ cup (125 ml) coconut cream
3 tablespoons Mussaman Curry Paste
  (page 23)
1 teaspoon oil
1 lb (500 g) beef sirloin
2 cups (500 ml) thin coconut milk
5 cardamom seeds, dry-roasted until
  fragrant
1 cinnamon stick, about 3 in (8 cm) in
  length
2 medium-sized potatoes (about 7 oz/
  200 g), peeled and cut into chunks
1 heaped tablespoon unsalted
  peanuts, chopped
5–10 shallots
3 bay leaves
2 tablespoons chopped palm sugar
2 tablespoons fish sauce
3 tablespoons tamarind juice
  (page 21)
Sweet and Spicy Pickled Vegetables
  (page 39)

1 Heat the coconut cream in a saucepan over medium heat, add the Mussaman Curry Paste, reduce heat to low and simmer for 5 minutes. Turn off heat and set aside.
2 Heat oil in a large pot or wok, then add the beef and stir-fry for 8–10 minutes, until almost cooked. Add the coconut milk and bring to a boil. Reduce heat to low and simmer gently for 10 minutes.
3 Add all the remaining ingredients and cook until the potatoes and meat are tender. Serve accompanied by Sweet and Spicy Pickled Vegetables (page 39) and rice.

Note: The potatoes provide a contrast in texture and a bland counterpoint to the spicy gravy.

Serves 4–6   Preparation time: 15 mins   Cooking time: 30 mins

Red Pork Curry   Gaeng Ped Moo

Pork is the most popular meat in Thailand, prepared in many different ways. This is a very simple, quickly prepared curry.

$1/2$ cup (125 ml) coconut cream
1 tablespoon Red Curry Paste
  (page 22)
12 oz (350 g) pork tenderloin (pork
  fillet), cut in bite-sized slices
$1/3$ cup (90 ml) pea-sized eggplants
  (optional)
$1^1/2$ cups (375 ml) thin coconut milk
$1^1/2$ tablespoons fish sauce
1 teaspoon sugar
5 kaffir lime leaves, halved
1 fresh red chili, thinly sliced
$1/2$ cup (20 g) Thai basil leaves
  (*horapa*)

1 Bring the coconut cream to a boil in a saucepan over medium heat, stirring constantly. Add the Red Curry Paste, pork, eggplant and coconut milk. Stir well and simmer over low heat until done, about 15 minutes.
2 Add the fish sauce, sugar, kaffir lime leaves and chili. Stir and heat through, then remove from heat and garnish with basil.

Note: If pork tenderloin is not available, use any other lean cut of pork.

Serves 4   Preparation time: 15 mins   Cooking time: 30 mins

Beef with Roasted Eggplant

Pla Nuea Makreua Orn

Although freshly grilled beef is delightful when used for this dish, it is also an ideal way to use up any leftover roast or steak.

8 oz (225 g) Asian eggplants
3 tablespoons oil
10 oz (300 g) uncooked or cooked beef steak
3 shallots, sliced
$^1/_2$ cup mint leaves or coriander leaves (cilantro)

Sauce
2–5 bird's-eye chilies, sliced
2 tablespoons lime juice
1$^1/_2$ tablespoons fish sauce
1 teaspoon sugar

1 Roast the eggplants under a broiler or on a grill, turning frequently, until the skins are blackened on all sides and the flesh is soft inside. Slice the eggplants in half, scoop out the flesh, discard the skins, and set aside.
2 If using uncooked beef, add 1 tablespoon of oil to the pan and sauté the steak over high heat until brown on both sides, about 3 minutes.
3 Fry the shallots in a separate pan in 2 tablespoons of oil over medium heat until brown and crisp, about 2 minutes. Drain and set aside.
4 Thinly slice the beef steak, combine with the eggplant and the Sauce ingredients, and mix well. Top with the fried shallots and serve at room temperature with white rice.

Note: If Asian eggplants are unavailable, Mediterranean eggplants may be used. Cut the eggplants into bite-sized pieces and stir-fry in 2 tablespoons of oil over high heat in a skillet or wok.

Serves 4   Preparation time: 15 mins   Cooking time: 25 mins

Chicken Stir-fried with Chili and Basil

Kha Kob Phad Ped

This dish is normally prepared with chicken but frogs' legs can also be used. Frogs, found in the klongs or canals and rice paddies of Thailand, are sometimes euphemistically called "paddy chickens." Their flavor is delicate and similar to chicken.

1 tablespoon oil
10 oz (300 g) boneless chicken thighs, deboned and cut into bite-sized chunks
  or frogs' legs, cleaned and skinned
1 tablespoon green peppercorns
2–3 red chilies, sliced lengthwise
3 in (8 cm) young galangal root, julienned
2 teaspoons fish sauce
$1/2$ teaspoon chopped palm sugar or dark brown sugar
Large handful Thai basil leaves (*horapa*)

1 Heat the oil in a wok until very hot. Add chicken chunks or frogs' legs and peppercorns and stir-fry over high heat for a couple of minutes. Add chilies, galangal, fish sauce and sugar. Mix well and cook for another minute. Stir in the basil and remove from the heat.
2 Serve accompanied by rice.

Serves 4   Preparation time: 15 mins   Cooking time: 15 mins

Barbecued Chicken Gai Yang

A northeastern version of a dish now served all over the country.

1 chicken (about 2¹/₄ lbs/1 kg), cut in
  serving pieces
1 tablespoon julienned ginger,
  for garnish

Marinade
10 cloves garlic, minced
1–2 tablespoons black peppercorns,
  crushed
2 tablespoons soy sauce
2 tablespoons sugar
2 tablespoons brandy or dry sherry
1 teaspoon salt

Sweet Thai Chili Sauce
¹/₂ cup distilled white vinegar
¹/₂ cup (100 g) sugar
5 cloves garlic, minced
2–3 red chilies, pounded or minced
¹/₂ teaspoon salt

1 Mix the Marinade ingredients in a bowl. Add the chicken and combine thoroughly with the Marinade. Set aside in the refrigerator for 3–4 hours.
2 Grill chicken over hot charcoal or under a broiler, turning from time to time until browned on all sides, about 25–30 minutes.
3 Meanwhile, mix all the Sweet Thai Chili Sauce ingredients in a saucepan, bring to a boil and simmer until the sauce thickens slightly. The sauce should have a thin, syrupy consistency. Set aside to cool.
4 Serve the chicken and Sweet Thai Chili Sauce accompanied by plain or glutinous rice and Green Papaya Salad (page 48).

Note: Sweet Thai Chilli Sauce is widely available bottled.

Serves 4   Preparation time: 15 mins   Cooking time: 30 mins

Grilled Pork with Chili Sauce Kaw Moo Yang

The common Thai seasonings of garlic, black pepper and coriander root are partnered with Chinese oyster sauce and soy sauce to marinate the pork, which is then grilled and served with a spicy sauce.

1¼ lbs (600 g) pork ribs, pork loin or pork neck, which is the traditional cut for this recipe

Marinade
2 tablespoons crushed garlic
1 tablespoon crushed coriander root
½ teaspoon freshly ground black pepper
2 tablespoons oyster sauce
2 tablespoons soy sauce
1 tablespoon sugar

Chili Sauce
6 shallots, thinly sliced
3 teaspoons chili flakes or ground red pepper
1½ tablespoons fish sauce
3 tablespoons lime juice

1 Separate the ribs or slice the pork into 1½-in (4-cm) strips. Mix all the Marinade ingredients together and marinate the pork for 1 hour.
2 While the pork is marinating, mix the Chili Sauce ingredients together and set aside.
3 Grill the pork over hot charcoal or under a very hot broiler for 15–20 minutes on each side, or until each side of the meat is browned.
4 If using pork loin, slice thinly. Place ribs or pork slices on a serving dish, and serve with the Chili Sauce accompanied by steamed glutinous rice and sliced cucumber.

Serves 4–6   Preparation time: 10 mins   Cooking time: 40–50 mins

Dry Beef Curry   Panaeng Nuea

A southern style of cooking beef, hot and fragrant with typicaly Indian spices. The use of palm sugar, peanuts and kaffir lime leaves, however, is distinctly Thai.

1 tablespoon coriander seeds and 2 teaspoons cumin seeds, ground in a mortar and pestle or spice grinder
3 tablespoons Mussaman Curry Paste (page 23)
$^1/_2$ cup (125 ml) coconut cream
12 oz (350 g) beef sirloin, cut into thin strips
$1^1/_2$ cups (375 ml) thin coconut milk
$^1/_2$ cup (90 g) roasted peanuts, crushed
$1^1/_2$–2 tablespoons fish sauce
3 tablespoons chopped palm sugar or dark brown sugar
6 kaffir lime leaves, torn in half
1 red chili, thinly sliced

1 Mix the ground coriander and cumin with the Mussaman Curry Paste. Heat coconut cream in a large pot or wok until some of the oil surfaces. Add the curry paste, reduce heat and slowly bring to a boil, stirring constantly.
2 Put in beef strips and cook for 5 minutes, then add coconut milk and the rest of ingredients, except for the kaffir lime leaves and chili. Simmer over low heat for 30 minutes, stirring frequently, until the meat is tender, and the oil has come out of the coconut milk.
3 Add the kaffir lime leaves and chili, remove from the heat and serve with white rice.

Serves 4   Preparation time: 15 mins   Cooking time: 40 mins

Stir-fried Squid with Garlic Pla Muk Tod

Despite its simplicity and speed of preparation, this is an absolutely delicious way of cooking squid.

1 lb (500 g) fresh squid
2 tablespoons oil
$1/2$ cup (100 g) minced garlic
1 teaspoon black peppercorns, crushed
1 tablespoon oyster sauce
$1/2$ tablespoon soy sauce
1 teaspoon fish sauce
1 teaspoon sugar
Coriander leaves (cilantro) to garnish

1 Remove the tentacles from the squid and cut out and discard the hard beak portion. Remove the skin from the body of the squid. Butterfly the squid by making a legthwise cut along the body of the squid. Clean inside and score the flesh by making diagonal criss-cross slits across the surface. This allows the squid to cook very quickly inside without becoming rubbery. Slice into bite-sized pieces. Dry thoroughly and set aside.
2 Heat the oil in a wok over medium heat. Fry the garlic until golden-brown, then add the squid and its tentacles, together with the seasonings. Stir-fry for 3–4 minutes, stirring constantly until the squid turns white or starts to curl. Do not overcook. Serve hot sprinkled with coriander leaves.

Note: Be sure to use fresh and not frozen squid, as the latter exudes water when cooked, making it stew rather than fry.

Serves 4   Preparation time 20 minutes   Cooking time 7 mins

Shrimp in Spicy Coconut Chu Chee Goong Lai

A curry-like dish in which the shrimp are cooked in a spicy coconut milk gravy that gains flavor from the addition of basil. Although large tiger prawns (about 6 per lb) are normally used, smaller prawns or shrimp may be substituted.

1 lb (500 g) fresh shrimp or prawns
$1/_2$ cup (125 ml) coconut cream
2 tablespoons Red Curry Paste (page 22)
1 cup (250 ml) thin coconut milk
$1/_2$ tablespoon fish sauce or to taste
1 tablespoon chopped palm sugar or dark brown sugar
2 kaffir lime leaves, very thinly sliced
Thai basil (*horapa*) or coriander leaves (cilantro) to garnish
2–3 red chilies, thinly sliced

1 Peel and devein the shrimp, discarding the heads and tails.
2 Heat the coconut cream in a large saucepan or wok over medium heat, add the curry paste and cook, stirring constantly, until fragrant, about 5 minutes.
3 Add the shrimp and coconut milk, and bring gently to a boil. Simmer over low heat for about 10 minutes or until shrimp are just cooked.
4 Season to taste with fish sauce and palm sugar.
5 Place shrimp on a serving platter garnished with shreds of kaffir lime leaves, basil and chilies.

Serves 4   Preparation time: 15 mins   Cooking time: 15 mins

Crabs with Glass Noodles in Claypot · Poo Ob Woon Sen

Cooking in a claypot is southern Chinese in origin. One popular version in Thailand uses either crab claws or whole crabs cut into serving pieces. Although slices of pork fat are normally used, bacon improves the flavor of an already tasty dish.

2 whole crabs (about 2 lbs/1kg)
1 tablespoon oil
7 cloves garlic, peeled and left whole
2 slices lean bacon, cut into 1-in (2$^1/_2$-cm) pieces
2 coriander roots, cut in half
2 in (5 cm) ginger, sliced
1 teaspoon white peppercorns, crushed
8 oz (250 g) dried glass noodles (bean threads or cellophane noodles) soaked in cold water to soften for 5 minutes and drained
1 teaspoon butter
1 tablespoon soy sauce
2 spring onions, cut in 1$^1/_2$-in (4-cm) lengths
1 sprig coriander leaves (cilantro)

Stock
2 cups (500 ml) Thai Chicken Stock (page 23)
2 tablespoons oyster sauce
1 tablespoon soy sauce
2 teaspoons fish sauce
1 teaspoon sesame oil
2 teaspoons brandy or whisky
2 teaspoons sugar

1 Place all the Stock ingredients in a pan, bring to a boil and simmer for 5 minutes. Remove from the heat and set aside to cool.

2 Clean each crab by scrubbing it briskly with a brush. (If still alive, make sure the pincers are tied securely.) Rinse well with cold water. Using a cleaver or a heavy knife, cut the crab in half, then halve it again. Chop off the pincers, crack them and set aside. Remove the shell, scrape it out and set aside any roe.

3 Heat the oil in a large claypot or heatproof casserole. Stir-fry the garlic over high heat till lightly brown. Add bacon and stir-fry for one minute. Add crab, coriander roots, ginger and peppercorns. Stir-fry for 3 minutes.

4 Add glass noodles, butter, soy sauce and Stock. Mix well, cover and cook over high heat for 15–20 minutes or until crabs are cooked. Stir in spring onions and garnish with cilantro. Serve hot.

Note: Lobsters or prawns may be substituted for the crabs. If using prawns, use 1 cup of Thai Chicken Stock instead of 2, and cook for only 10–15 minutes.

Serves 4   Preparation time: 45 mins   Cooking time: 25 mins

Charcoal-grilled Prawns with Sweet and Sour Sauce   Goong Pow

The fragrance of fresh seafood grilling over charcoal is irresistible. In Thailand, this dish is made with huge fresh-water prawns. Tiger prawns, crayfish or lobsters may be used instead.

2–3 lbs (1–1^1/$_4$ kg) prawns, shrimp, crayfish or lobsters
Foil or banana leaf

Sweet and Sour Sauce
3 tablespoons tamarind pulp
^{1}/$_2$ cup water
2–3 tablespoons sugar
pinch of salt
1–2 tablespoons minced garlic
2–3 bird's-eye chilies or 1–2 red chilies, minced
1–2 teaspoons chopped fresh coriander leaves (cilantro)
1 teaspoon fish sauce
1 teaspoon lime juice (optional)

1 Prepare the Sweet and Sour Sauce first. In a bowl, mix the tamarind pulp with the water, mashing gently and removing any seeds and fibers. Transfer to a pan, add the sugar and bring to a boil. Lower the heat and simmer, stirring constantly until thick and syrupy. Turn off the heat, add the salt and stir well. Remove from heat and allow to cool, then strain the mixture. Add the remaining ingredients to the strained mixture and mix thoroughly.
2 Clean the prawns or crayfish and wrap each securely in foil or banana leaf. Grill over a hot charcoal fire or under a broiler for about 12 minutes.
3 Serve with the Sweet and Sour Sauce or Green Chili Sauce (page 22).

Serves 4   Preparation time: 15 mins   Cooking time: 30 mins

Deep-fried Stuffed Crab in the Shell   Poo Jaa

Use either mud crabs or blue swimmer crabs for this dish. The filling can be prepared in advance and the crabs stuffed and deep-fried just before serving.

4 crab shells for stuffing
3 eggs, well beaten
5 cups (1 1/4 liters) oil for deep-frying
1 tablespoon minced coriander
  leaves (cilantro)
2 red chilies for garnish

Stuffing
6 oz (175 g) ground pork
1/2 cup fresh shrimp or prawn meat,
  minced
1/2 cup (60 g) fresh crabmeat
1 tablespoon finely minced onion
1 tablespoon minced spring onions
1 teaspoon ground white pepper
1 teaspoon sugar
1/4 teaspoon soy sauce
1/4 teaspoon salt

1 Mix all the Stuffing ingredients together and fill the crab shells.
2 Heat the oil in a deep saucepan, dip the stuffed crabs in the beaten egg to coat them well all over and then deep-fry for about 10–15 minutes until cooked.
3 Remove from the heat and drain on paper towels. Sprinkle with coriander leaves (cilantro) and chilies before serving.

Note: If using cooked crabs, remove the backs carefully and discard any spongy matter. Wash backs and set aside. Remove crabmeat from body, legs and claws and measure out 1/2 cup (60 g), keeping the rest aside for another dish. If using raw crabs, steam first, then prepare as directed above.

Serves 4   Preparation time: 15 mins   Cooking time: 15 mins

Clams with Basil and Prawn Chili Paste   Hoy Lai Pedi

Use any type of clams for this emphatic, quickly prepared dish. It's worth hunting for Thai basil (*horapa*), as it makes a definite difference to the flavor of the clams.

3 tablespoons oil
2 lbs (1 kg) clams in their shells, soaked and cleaned well
2 tablespoons minced garlic
2–3 fresh red chilies, sliced length-wise
3 tablespoons Prawn Chili Paste (page 22)
2 teaspoons soy sauce
$^1/_2$ cup (125 ml) Thai Chicken Stock (page 23)
Large handful of Thai basil leaves (*horapa*)

1 Heat the oil in a wok over high heat, add the clams and garlic and stir-fry for 2–3 minutes until the clams open slightly. Add the fresh chilies, Prawn Chili Paste and soy sauce, stir well, then add Thai Chicken Stock. Simmer for 5 minutes. Scoop out the clams and leave the stock in the wok to simmer on high heat for 3–5 minutes.
2 Add the basil and pour the sauce over the clams.
3 Serve immediately, accompanied by rice.

Note: Soak the clams in several changes of water for $^1/_2$ hour or so before cooking to ensure they are thoroughly clean.

Serves 4–6   Preparation time: 10 mins   Cooking time: 12 mins

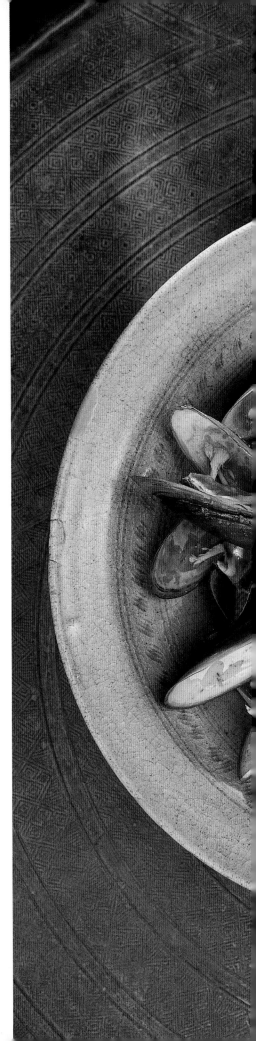

Steamed Mussels with Basil
Hoi Ma-Laeng Poo Ob

Beautiful orange-fleshed, green-lipped mussels contrast with bright green basil leaves in this simple but excellent seafood dish.

4 lbs (2 kg) mussels, soaked and cleaned well
Large handful Thai basil leaves (*horapa*)

Dipping Sauce
$1/_2$ cup (125 ml) freshly squeezed lime juice
2 tablespoons fish sauce
1 teaspoon sugar
2 coriander roots, chopped
2 cloves garlic, crushed
$1/_2$ cup (125 ml) water

1 Place the mussels in a steamer over boiling water and sprinkle with basil leaves. Steam for 10 minutes or until all mussels are cooked and open. Remove from the heat and wait for 2 minutes before opening the steamer.
2 Meanwhile, mix the Dipping Sauce ingredients together, bring to a boil, then set aside to cool.
3 Serve the mussels accompanied by the Dipping Sauce.

Note: Leaving the mussels to sit covered for a couple of minutes after steaming helps the flavor of basil to permeate the mussels.

Serves 4   Preparation time: 10 mins   Cooking time: 15 mins

Crispy Fried Catfish with Green Mango Salad   Pla Samlee Dad Deow

The sour tang of unripe green mangoes mixed with other seasonings enhances the flavor of fresh fried fish. Use any firm-textured white fish. (Catfish fillets best approximate the flavor of the cottonfish used in Thailand for this dish.)

10 oz (300 g) freshwater catfish or
    fish fillets
2 cups (500 ml) oil for deep-frying

Green Mango Salad
2–3 small green unripe mangoes,
    peeled and grated to yield 1 cup
5–7 shallots, sliced
2–3 bird's-eye chilies, thinly sliced
1–2 tablespoons shaved palm sugar
    or dark brown sugar
1 teaspoon fish sauce
1 teaspoon lime juice
3 tablespoons roasted cashew nuts,
    or 2 tablespoons crushed peanuts,
    to garnish

1 Clean and scale the fish, removing the head. Cut lengthwise from underneath and carefully remove the backbone and all other bones. Dry thoroughly and set aside.
2 Mix together all ingredients for the Green Mango Salad. Taste and add a little fish sauce if not sufficiently salty; if not sour enough, add more lime juice.
3 Deep-fry the fish in hot oil until crisp and golden.
4 Drain and serve the fish with the Green Mango Salad arranged in the center. Sprinkle with roasted cashew nuts or crushed peanuts.

Serves 4   Preparation time: 20 mins   Cooking time: 10 mins

Fried Fish with Chili Shrimp Paste Sauce Pla Nuea Orn

Although freshwater fish are preferred for this dish in Thailand, any good white-fleshed fish may be used.

1 whole fish weighing about 2 lbs
  (1 kg), or 2 smaller fish
4 cups (1 liter) oil for deep-frying

Chili Shrimp Paste Sauce
5–10 dried red chilies, soaked in
  water, deseeded and finely
  chopped
$1/_2$ cup (100 g) minced garlic
$1/_2$ cup (100 g) sliced shallots
$1/_2$ tablespoon dried shrimp paste
3 tablespoons oil
1 teaspoon fish sauce
1 teaspoon sugar
4–5 kaffir lime leaves, very finely
  sliced

1 Scale and clean the fish thoroughly, leaving on the head. Make cuts about $1/_2$ in (1 cm) apart along the back of the fish to give it a decorative appearance.

2 To make the Chili Shrimp Paste Sauce, heat 3 tablespoons oil in a wok over high heat and fry the chilies, garlic, shallots and shrimp paste until fragrant, then add the fish sauce and sugar. Fry for another 1–2 minutes and set aside.

3 Dry the fish thoroughly, then deep-fry in very hot oil until cooked. Serve the fish topped with the Chili Shrimp Paste Sauce and sprinkled with shredded kaffir lime leaves.

Serves 4   Preparation time: 30 mins   Cooking time: 12 mins

Crispy Fish Fillets with Red Curry Sauce
Pla Chorn Phad Prik Khing

Pla chorn, a fish that is similar to Spanish mackerel, is preferred for this recipe, in which fish fillets are fried until crisp and topped with a thick, spicy sauce. Any firm-textured white fish can be used.

12 oz (350 g) fish fillets or steaks, cut into bite-sized chunks
Oil for deep frying
1 cup long or green beans, cut in bite-sized lengths
1 kaffir lime leaf, very thinly sliced

Red Curry Sauce
2 tablespoons Red Curry Paste (page 22)
$^{1}/_{2}$ cup (125 ml) thick coconut milk
1 teaspoon fish sauce
1 teaspoon sugar
2 tablespoons dried prawns or shrimp, soaked in warm water for 10 minutes, drained, and ground in a blender or mortar and pestle

1 Dry the fish thoroughly, then deep-fry in very hot oil until crisp and golden. Set aside.
2 To make the Red Curry Sauce, mix the curry paste with the coconut milk in a saucepan and cook over medium heat, stirring continuously until the sauce thickens. Then add the fish sauce, sugar and dried prawns or shrimp.
3 To serve, put the crispy fish on a plate. Top with the sauce and scatter with long beans or green beans and sliced kaffir lime leaf.

Serves 4   Preparation time: 15 mins   Cooking time: 45 mins

Red Ruby Chestnut Morsels in Sweet Coconut   Tab Tim Grob

1 cup (200 g) diced water
   chestnut morsels
Few drops red food coloring (optional)
1/2 cup (60 g) tapioca starch
   (tapioca flour)
5 cups (11/4 liters) water
Crushed ice

Sweet Coconut Milk
1/2 cup (100 g) sugar
3/4 cup (180 ml) water
3/4 cup (180 ml) thick coconut milk

Serves 4–6   Preparation time: 20 mins
Cooking time: 8 mins

1 Sprinkle the water chestnut morsels with a few drops of red food coloring and toss until bright red. Put the tapioca starch in a plastic bag, add water chestnuts and shake until thoroughly coated.
2 Put the water chestnut morsels and tapioca starch in a colander or sieve and shake until excess flour falls away. Bring 5 cups water to a boil in a pot. Add the water chestnut morsels and simmer for 3 minutes. Drain water chestnuts and plunge into cold water. Drain again and set aside.
3 To make the Sweet Coconut Milk, boil the sugar and water in a saucepan over high heat for 3 minutes. Set aside to cool, then add the coconut milk and stir.
4 To serve, put a little of the water chestnut rubies into dessert dishes and add some of the Sweet Coconut Milk and crushed ice. Additional slices of ripe jackfruit or young coconut may be added if these are available.

Bananas in Coconut Milk   Kloey Buad Chee

2 cups (500 ml) thin coconut milk
1/4 cup (100 g) sugar
1/4 teaspoon salt
8 small or 4 large ripe bananas, cut
   diagonally in slices

Serves 4   Preparation time: 10 mins
Cooking time: 10 mins

1 Pour the coconut milk into a saucepan, then add the sugar and salt. Bring gently to a boil over low heat, stirring constantly to prevent the coconut milk from separating.
2 Add the bananas, and cook over low heat for 5 minutes. Remove from the heat and serve hot or cold.

Glutinous Rice Beads in Coconut Milk   Bua Loi

11/2 cups (370 g) glutinous rice flour
3/4 cup (180 ml) water
Few drops food coloring (optional)
2 cups (500 ml) thick coconut milk
1 cup (200 g) sugar
1 teaspoon salt

Serves 4–6   Preparation time: 30 mins
Cooking time: 10 mins

1 Mix the glutinous rice flour with the water to make a stiff paste. Knead well. If using coloring, divide the dough into two batches, add a few drops of coloring to each batch and mix well. Roll dough into long noodle-like strips. Pinch off bits from the strips and form into pea-sized balls. Bring a large pot of water to a boil, toss in the balls and remove when they float to the surface. Drain.
2 Bring half the coconut milk and sugar to a boil over low heat, stirring constantly to prevent it from separating, then add the cooked rice flour beads. When the mixture returns to a boil, remove from the heat and stir in the remaining coconut milk. Serve in small bowls.

Note: If you cannot obtain glutinous rice flour, you can make the paste directly from glutinous rice. To make the paste, soak 11/2 cups glutinous rice in water for 5 hours. Drain and transfer the rice to a blender. Add 3/4 cup water and grind till a thick liquid mixture forms. Pour the mixture into a fine muslin cloth and drain until the water is gone. Knead the remaining paste to form a dough, adding small amounts of water if needed.
You may add canned sweet corn kernels and cooked, colored diced water chestnut (prepared as for Red Rubies, see above) to this dish for a more varied and colorful dessert.

Steamed Pumpkin Custard Sangkaya Fak Thong

A visually intriguing dessert where a rich coconut-milk custard is steamed inside a small pumpkin or acorn squashes.

5 eggs (2 of them duck eggs if possible)
1 cup (250 ml) coconut cream
1 cup (150 g) chopped palm sugar or dark brown sugar
1 small pumpkin, about 8 in (20 cm) in diameter, or 2 acorn squashes

1 Beat the eggs with coconut cream and sugar until the mixture is frothy.
2 Cut the top off the pumpkin or acorn squashes and carefully scoop out the seeds and any fibers. Pour in the coconut cream mixture, cover with the top of the pumpkin or squashes and place in a steamer. Cover the steamer and place over boiling water.
3 Cook over medium heat for about 30 minutes or until the mixture has set. Leave to cool (preferably refrigerate) and cut in thick slices to serve.

Note: Duck eggs add richness and a firmer texture to the custard. If using palm sugar, strain the custard through a sieve before pouring into the pumpkin to remove any impurities.

Serves 4   Preparation time: 10 mins   Cooking time: 30 mins

Deep-fried Bananas with Coconut   Khao Mao Tod

These bananas are rolled in a mixture of grated coconut and palm sugar before being dipped in batter and deep-fried.

1 cup freshly grated coconut
$3/4$ cup (110 g) chopped palm sugar
14 small ripe finger bananas or 5–6
   large ripe bananas, sliced into 2–3
   sections
5 cups ($1^1/4$ liters) oil for deep-frying

Batter
2 cups (300 g) glutinous rice flour
1 cup (250 ml) thin coconut milk
$1/2$ cup (125 ml) water
1 egg, lightly beaten
1 tablespoon sesame seeds (optional)

1 Combine the coconut and palm sugar and cook for 15 minutes in a non-stick pan over low heat, stirring frequently. Set aside. Mix the Batter ingredients and let it stand for 3 hours.
2 Just before serving, heat oil in a deep saucepan, roll each banana in the coconut-palm sugar mixture, then dip in the batter and fry in very hot oil until golden brown. Serve hot.

Note: If you cannot obtain glutinous rice flour, substitute with glutinous rice paste that you make directly from glutinous rice grains. To make the paste, soak 2 cups of glutinous rice in water for 5 hours. Drain and transfer the rice to a blender. Add 1 cup of water and grind till a thick liquid forms. Pour the mixture into a fine muslin cloth and strain until the water is gone. Add the remaining rice flour paste to the other Batter ingredients, omitting the water. Mix and set aside to stand for 3 hours.

Serves 6   Preparation time: 15 mins   Cooking time: 50 mins

Steamed Glutinous Rice Cakes with Banana   Kao Tom Mad

$1^1/4$ cups (300 g) glutinous rice,
   soaked in water for 1 hour and
   drained
2 cups (500 ml) thick coconut milk
4 tablespoons sugar
Pinch of salt
$1/2$ cup (3 oz/100 g) dried red beans,
   soaked overnight then boiled in 3
   cups water until soft
4 small or 2 large ripe bananas,
   sliced
8 pieces banana leaf or aluminum
   foil, about 6 x 10 in (12 x 25 cm)

1 Mix the soaked, drained glutinous rice with coconut milk, sugar and salt in a nonstick saucepan and bring to a boil over medium heat. Reduce heat to low and simmer, stirring constantly until the rice is cooked and all the coconut milk absorbed. This should take about 15 minutes. Leave to cool.
2 Take a piece of banana leaf and put a tablespoon of the rice and a teaspoon of red beans on it. Place a slice of banana on top, cover with more rice and red beans, then fold up the banana leaf and secure with a toothpick. Repeat until all bananas are used up.
3 Steam for 25 minutes and set aside to cool.
4 Unwrap the banana leaves and serve.

Serves 8   Preparation time: 30 mins   Cooking time: 70 mins

Measurements and Conversion Tables

Measurements in this book are given in volume as far as possible. Teaspoon, tablespoon and cup measurements should be level, not heaped, unless otherwise indicated. Australian readers please note that the standard Australian measuring spoon is larger than the UK or American spoon by 5 ml, so use $^3/_4$ tablespoon instead of a full tablespoon when following the recipes.

Liquid Conversions

Imperial	Metric	US cups
$^1/_2$ fl oz	15 ml	1 tablespoon
1 fl oz	30 ml	$^1/_8$ cup
2 fl oz	60 ml	$^1/_4$ cup
4 fl oz	125 ml	$^1/_2$ cup
5 fl oz ($^1/_4$ pint)	150 ml	$^2/_3$ cup
6 fl oz	175 ml	$^3/_4$ cup
8 fl oz	250 ml	1 cup
12 fl oz	375 ml	$1^1/_2$ cups
16 fl oz	500 ml	2 cups

Note:
1 UK pint = 20 fl oz
1 US pint = 16 fl oz

Solid Weight Conversions

Imperial	Metric
$^1/_2$ oz	15 g
1 oz	30g
$1^1/2$ oz	50 g
2 oz	60 g
3 oz	90 g
$3^1/2$ oz	100 g
4 oz ($^1/_4$ lb)	125 g
5 oz	150 g
6 oz	185 g
7 oz	200 g
8 oz ($^1/_2$ lb)	250 g
9 oz	280 g
10 oz	300 g
16 oz (1 lb)	500 g
32 oz (2 lbs)	1 kg

Oven Temperatures

Heat	Fahrenheit	Centigrade/Celsius	British Gas Mark
Very cool	225	110	$^1/_4$
Cool or slow	275–300	135–150	1–2
Moderate	350	175	4
Hot	425	220	7
Very hot	450	230	8

Index of Recipes

Mail-order/Online Sources of Ingredients

The ingredients used in this book can all be found in markets featuring the foods of Southeast Asia. Many of them can also be found in any well-stocked supermarket. Ingredients not found locally may be available from the mail-order/online addresses listed below.

AsianWok.com
www.asianwok.com

Anzen Importers
736 NE Martin Luther King Blvd.
Portland, OR 97232
Tel: 503-233-5111

Bangkok Market
5815 Maywood Ave.
Maywood, CA 90270-2507
Tel: 323-585-5385
www.bangkokmarket.com

Central Market
4001 N Lamar Blvd.
Austin, Texas
Tel: 512-206-1000
www.centralmarket.com

Dekalb Farmers Market
3000 East Ponce De Leon Ave.
Decatur, GA 30030
Tel: 404-377-6400
www.dekalbfarmersmarket.com

Dean & Deluca
560 Broadway
New York, NY 10012
Tel: 212-226-6800
www.deandeluca.com

Erawan Market
1463 University Ave.
Berkeley, CA 94702
Tel: 510-849-9707

Gourmail, Inc.
816 Newtown Road
Berwyn, PA 19312
Tel: 800-442-2340

ImportFood.com
PO Box 2054
Issaquah, WA 98027
Tel: 425-392-7516
www.importfood.com

Kam Man Food Products
200 Canal Street
New York, NY 10013
Tel: 212-571-0330
www.kammanfood.com

Oriental Food Market and Cooking School, Inc.
2801 W. Howard St.
Chicago, IL 60645
Tel: 773-274-2826

Pacificrim-gourmet.com
4905 Morena Blvd., Suite 1313
San Diego, CA 92117
Tel: 858-274-9013
www.i-clipse.com

Penn Herb Co. Ltd.
603 North 2nd St.
Philadelphia, PA 19123
Tel: 800-523-9971
www.pennherb.com

Rafal Spice Company
2521 Russell St.
Detroit, MI 48207
Tel: 313-259-6373
www.rafalspicecompany.com

The Spice House
1048 N. Old World 3rd St.
Milwaukee, WI
Tel: 414-272-0977
www.thespicehouse.com

Temple of Thai
104 Mosco St.
New York, NY 10013
Tel: 877-519-0709
www.templeofthai.com

Thai Grocery
5014 N Broadway St.
Chicago, IL 60640
Tel: 773-561-5345

Uwajimaya
PO Box 3003
Seattle, WA 98114
Tel: 206-624-6248
www.uwajimaya.com

Hoo Hing
Freshwater Road, Chadwell Heath
Romfod, Essex RM8 1RX
Tel: 44-0-20-8548-3636
www.hoohing.com

Porter Foods Co. Ltd
24 Hockerill Court
London Road, Bishops Stortford
Hertfordshire CM23 5SB
Tel: 44-0-1279-501711
www.porter-foods.co.uk

Thai Taste
Tel: 0870-241-1960
www.thaitaste.co.uk